LAKE

ARAL SEA

U S S R

Syrdarya (Jaxartes)

(FERGHANA)

(TRANSOXIANA)

CASPIAN SEA

Amu-Darya (Oxus)

• Bukhara
• Samarkand

• Tabriz

AFGHANISTAN

KASHMIR

Qazvin •
• Mashhad

• Teheran
• Kirmanshah
(KHURASAN)
• Kabul

ris

• Kashan
• Herat

Srinagar •
• Achabal

marra
• Baghdad
IRAN
Verinag •

• Susa
Isfahan •

Lahore •

IRAQ

Euphrates

• Pasargadae
PAKISTAN
• Kandahar

Panipat •

• Persepolis
• Kerman

Delhi •
• Sikandra

Shiraz
• Mahan

Fathpur Sikri •
• Agra

Indus

• Ajmer

Ganga (Ganges)

Udaipur •

Gujarat

Narmada

SAUDI ARABIA

ecca

• Aurangabad

ARABIAN SEA
INDIA

GARDENS OF PARADISE

GARDENS OF PARADISE

The History and Design
of the Great Islamic Gardens

JOHN BROOKES

New Amsterdam
New York

First published in the United States of America in 1987 by
The Meredith Press, by arrangement with
Weidenfeld and Nicolson, London.

Designed by Helen Lewis

Library of Congress Cataloging-in-Publication Data

Brookes, John, 1933–
  Gardens of paradise.

  Bibliography: p.
  Includes index.
    1. Gardens, Islamic.   2. Gardens, Islamic – History.
  I. Title.
  SB 457.8. B76   1987   712'.6'09174927   87–12229
  ISBN 0–941533–07–7

New Amsterdam Books
The Meredith Press
171 Madison Avenue
New York, N.Y. 10016

TITLE PAGE ILLUSTRATION
*A cascade in the Shalamar Bagh, Kashmir, India. The recesses behind the waterfall,
which are shaped like a* mihrab *(niche in a mosque indicating
the direction of Mecca), hold cut dahlia heads.*

PICTURE ACKNOWLEDGMENTS

Photographs and illustrations were supplied by the author except
for those which came from the following sources:

British Library 12, 14, 18, 71, 73, 120, 121, 169, 171, 187; J. Allan Cash 165;
P. Coste, *Architecture Arabe: Monuments du Kaire*, Paris 1839: 179, 181B;
P. Coste, *Monuments Modernes de la Perse*, Paris 1867: 80T, 83B, 86, 108;
Description de L'Egypte: Etat Moderne, Planches I, Paris 1809: 180, 181T;
Dr James Dickie 46, 102T; E. Flandin, *Voyage en Perse 1840–41: Perse Moderne*,
Paris 1843–54: 83T, 106; Werner Forman Archive 99, 175B;
Colin Grant 43T, 43B, 51, 53L, 57, 59, 63, 68, 97T, 97B, 98, 100;
Edward Grant 166; Robert Harding Picture Library 91; E. Herzfeld,
Erster Vorläufiger Bericht über die Ausgrabungen von Samarra, Berlin 1912: 36;
C. John Rare Rugs Ltd 20; J. de Morgan, *Mission Scientifique en Perse* IV pt 2,
Paris 1897: 34L; A. U. Pope (ed.), *A Survey of Persian Art* I, London 1938: 33;
Frank Spooner Pictures 101 (photo A. Hutt); Victoria and Albert Museum
(by courtesy of the Board of Trustees) 117, 123, 126, 129R, 170, 202;
Weidenfeld and Nicolson Archives 25, 53R, 61T, 61B, 80B, 134, 135,
153, 161, 164, 180, 185, 186T, 186B, 189, 197, 198, 201.

Maps and plans were also provided by the author except for those on the endpapers,
27T, 34R and 49T, which were produced by DP Press.

CONTENTS

AUTHOR'S ACKNOWLEDGMENTS

I would especially like to thank the late Antony Hutt for introducing me to Islamic culture, then guiding me, under the auspices of Thomas Swann, round the archaeological sites of Iran, later accompanying me to the south of Spain, and lastly for providing invaluable advice on some aspects of this book. I would also like to thank Hossain Rafi and his family, who took me under their wing during very difficult times; Philip Ward-Green, who accompanied me on my Tehran walks; and my Iranian students, who, I think, were unaware that they were revealing to me much of contemporary Shi'ite Muslim life and thought.

My thanks are also due to Inder Jit, who smoothed my way in India, and to Brigadier Peter Thwaites in Oman. John Kelsey, Maurice Lee, John H. Harvey and Yusuf Mardin have also provided me with information on the Middle East and Turkey, for which I am most grateful. Further thanks go to Miss Felicity Miles for her many hours spent typing on my behalf.

Lastly I would like to thank the many knowing, and unknowing, over whose walls and through whose gates I peered to see and photograph their own particular version of earthly paradise.

JOHN BROOKES
Sussex, May 1987

FOREWORD

The influence of Islam on the artistic development of the Muslim is undoubted. Art emerged as a manifestation of religion: singing and music, sculpture and architecture, poetry and prose all have their genesis in the religious life of man. Islam not only fostered these artistic talents but also influenced their direction. Fearing that man might lapse into his old habit of attributing to statues heavenly authority, it prohibited the portraying of live objects in stone and even, according to some scholars, on canvas. The development of Muslim art, therefore, followed a different direction from that of its Western counterpart. The visual expression of beauty was manifested in geometrical designs of an exceptionally beautiful and intricate nature. It was also manifested in magnificent Islamic buildings that have influenced the development of architecture throughout the world. Calligraphy was a rich substitute for pictures and drawing as known in the West. These aspects of Muslim art are widely recognized and consequently well served by scholarship.

One Muslim contribution to the beauty of nature which has so far received little attention is the art of landscaping and gardening. Perhaps the explanation for this neglect is that most of those who worked in Islamic art or architecture were generally archaeologists or historians whose perception of buildings was immediate and informed, but whose perception of the beauty of landscaping, the charm of scattered plants and flowers, and the magic of the mixtures of colour in a garden, was limited. Yet the world has a great deal to learn from the Muslim art of landscaping. Just as Muslim architecture is unique, so is Muslim gardening and landscaping. Muslim building emphasizes light and space – the Muslim garden, on the other hand, celebrates the sound of water flowing from various directions, and shrubs and trees are scattered with studied carelessness to beautify nature without violating it, to emphasize its spirit rather than suppress it. It is this spirit of harmony with nature that is the most obvious characteristic of the Muslim garden.

In this book Mr Brookes has brought to life this neglected field of Muslim culture. He has delved into many references and, as a gardener, has visited many Muslim gardens all over the world, examining them with his expert eye and describing them with skill and thoroughness.

As a Muslim it makes me proud to read about the Islamic art of landscaping and gardening as presented by a professional gardener who has written about his subject with the tender care usually reserved for rare plants. This is a great contribution to the study of the art and culture of Islam.

DR M. A. ZAKI BADAWI
Principal of the Muslim College, London

INTRODUCTION

I was fortunate to have seen Iran during its quieter moments, although my stay there overlapped with the beginnings of the revolution in late 1978. The uncertainty of that extraordinary period, of not knowing what lay ahead, made me doubly conscious of the landscape and its unfolding seasons.

As an antidote to the political upheavals and the absence of departed friends, I took solace in the countryside, the scale and diversity of which is magnificent. Its timeless quality makes you aware of the superficiality of yet another period of upheaval upon the broad back of this landscape which for centuries has had to support waves of migrant tribes, Mongol hordes and despotic imperial dynasties. Yet those vast tracts of land – some dry desert, some green valleys and some humid forest – have not changed; and still, within the environs of present-day Tehran, lonely shepherds herd flocks of sheep and goats which devour all before them as they have done for a thousand years. These nibbling menaces have changed the face of the Middle East far more than the ravages of man.

Quite near my home above Tehran was a deep valley, fed by rushing waters from the adjacent mountains. In this secluded place I walked most weekends, if not exploring further afield, and experienced the Persian year at 900 metres: first, a golden autumn, with white colchicums under colouring groves of pomegranate trees, russet poplars and mellowing mulberries; then winter, with the ribbed grey trunks of walnut trees and blotched stems of *chenar*, or plane trees, outlined against massive grey

OPPOSITE BELOW *A typical valley (and potential garden location) in the foothills of the Alborz Mountains north of Tehran, Iran. The trees are mainly walnut and pomegranate.*

ABOVE *Flocks of sheep and goats still wander over much of the Middle East,
devouring all before them, as they have done for thousands of years.*

stone walls, set up to retain the terrace gardens. For the valley was a series of terraced levels growing fruit and vegetables, descending in steps to the stream along the valley floor. A lone cypress rose out of a deserted orchard. In spring, successive waves of almond, cherry, apple, pear and medlar blossom gave way to the first green tufts of ailanthus, followed by the new shoots of walnut and chenar, the whole offset by the extraordinary intensity of young pomegranate foliage.

Beneath the fruit trees on the fertile valley floor, small areas were levelled, and blocked water channels, arranged in a grid-iron pattern, were opened to irrigate the gardens under the trees in which vegetables were grown. In these uncultivated plots a million wild flowers appear, of stronger colours than those of European meadows and often the original forms of our cultivated garden species. On the shady banks of the valley, the Persian rose grows in drifts, following early spring bulbs, blue muscari, vivid blue ixiolirion and the odd wild tulip. Within the long grass, cornflowers, poppies, wild borage and gladioli are to be found. As summer proceeds, the flowers fade and, as the overhead canopy thickens to fruiting, sheep and goats are herded through the valley.

Into this colourful place each weekend, family picnickers bring piles of food and samovars which are laid out on carpets amongst the greenery. Groups of eight and ten take up their positions quite early in the day and stay till dusk, their songs and chatter mixing with the rush of the stream

Like a scene from a Persian miniature, men sit smoking a waterpipe on a carpet in the shade of some chenar trees.

and the trill and gurgle of overhead nightingales and rollers. Bright king-fishers dart about the stream's edge.

It is with this scene in mind that one should try to understand the origins of the Persian garden for, if this abundance did not grow naturally, it was created, or at least aspired to. Although the early geometric form of the garden was dictated by the practicalities of the irrigational system, three sources were used to guide the garden-builder in his quest for this ideal of the perfect paradise garden: miniature paintings, depictions in imaginative writings and the Quran itself.

The Mongol hordes first pitched their tents in such a garden and held their courts in such a place, later introducing open pavilions set about the garden. As in my valley, streams which once irrigated the valley bottom alone became controlled and organized to irrigate further afield, while still fulfilling their early task. The original scattered trees became an orchard within the scheme. In myth and literature, the garden became a metaphor for coolness and plenty among bright flowers, and individual aspects of the scene take on other significances which provide a guide to the Muslim way of life. For water, sun and shade and burgeoning nature are a basic common point of reference. Even in post-revolutionary Iran, it is the tulip that symbolizes the dawning of a new era.

The richness of a fleeting spring, its coolness before the summer heat, the abundance of mountain waters after the thaw, all are still a wonder to the average Persian. I believe it is this timeless wonder, encapsulated in manuscripts and the printed word, which has made the garden, if not the central pivot of the Muslim world, at least a continuing verdant background to it.

The romantic in most of us in the West cannot be unaware of the allure of the so-called Eastern garden. This awareness was fostered by nineteenth-century watercolourists, by travellers' tales and the ubiquitous quotations and ornamented writings of the Persian poet Omar Khayyam, whose *Rubaiyat* was popularized in the rendering of Edward Fitzgerald.

In the West, the garden is traditionally a place for extrovert show, some measure of which still exists in the extent to which we elaborate our mean suburban plots; but the oriental garden, recalled in a thousand legends, glimpsed in miniatures and portrayed in Hollywood epics, was voluptuous, a total sensual experience plucking the heart-strings and titillating the senses of sound, touch, sight and smell. It was, and still is, a private place,

پیش ایشان و حال سلطان روم معلوم کنم چون آمدند که روی بدیشان دارد بایدی که گفتند و دشنام و داد و خوش

نباشد ما میری مصرعی بگویم که چهارم را قافیه نباشد چون بیاید بگویم رفیقیم ما کنیم تا این بای را تمام

کند چون شما بندرید و بدین اتفاق کرد بندین جون فسرو و سی سلام کرد و جواب یافت و آمدند بر سد که از کجایی گفت ازقصبه

طوس و حال ایشان بگفت و حال سلطان استفسار کرد ایشان گفتند ما فلان و فلان و فلان و امرو خلوت

آمده ایم و هر یکی مصرعی گفتیم و مقرر است که هر مصرع چهارم تمام کند رفیق ماست و العیش ما موفق گفت و فردوسی

گفت بگویید اگر توانم گفت کویم و آن رخت بر هم عنصری گفت

چون عارض تو ماه نباشد روشن | فردوسی گفت

مانند رخ گل بود در گلشن | عسجدی گفت
مژگانت همی گذر کند از جوشن | فردوسی گفت

ماند سنان کیو در جنگ بشن

ایشان ایستادند و فرو ماندند که پیش که بود و جنگ او بود و چگونه بود و فردوسی

داستان جنگ بشن پیش ایشان بگفت هر که کشیده و بود ایشان را خوش آمد آخر الامر فردوسی کرد

از و روز را به عشرت با یکدیگر بسر بردند چون بندجون بشهر رفتند و هر یک گفت شه کو گذر دار و دیگری عصری

a retreat from the world, cool after the heat of the day, with bubbling waters, the rustle of breeze-blown silk and throbbing night-time scents, a place of total relaxation, unworldly its timelessness.

Such a creation lies at the heart of Islamic thought where it is more often an exercise in the mind's eye than the visible extravaganza we assume, for it has spiritual significance as the domestic version of that paradise towards which the Quran directs its disciples to strive as their reward for this life's hardships. Although not described in detail, many delights await the believer:

The gardens of Paradise shall be abounding in branches, therein fountains of running water, and of every fruit there shall be two kinds. The believers shall find themselves reclining upon couches lined with brocade, the fruits of the garden nigh to gather; and will find therein maidens restraining their glances, untouched before them by any man or Jinn, lovely as rubies, beautiful as coral.

And again,

There will be green, green pastures, therein fountains of running water, fruits and palm-trees, and pomegranates, maidens good and comely, houris cloistered in cool pavilions reclining upon green cushions, immortal youths who seem as if scattered pearls, adorned with brocades and bracelets of silver.

There are also descriptions of rich pavilions wherein the owners of the gardens might relax with their friends amongst orchards of laden fruit trees. The importance of water is also clearly stressed, for its significance in a harsh climate is not considered purely utilitarian.

These promised joys of paradise have to be seen in the context of grinding poverty for the majority, of great summer heat and of desert harshness with near-drought conditions. The physical sanctuary such a place offers, with its cooling shade and its sounds of water, is difficult for a European to grasp, if he has not experienced the high temperatures and suffocating summer dust of a desert climate. In her book *Passenger to Tehran* (1926), Vita Sackville-West describes her initial disappointment at not finding a Persian garden worthy of its reputation, but then slowly the realization dawns on her of the Islamic ideal, of the garden as a symbol of refuge. She records this awareness vividly:

Imagine you have ridden in summer for four days across a plain; that you have then come to a barrier of snow-mountains and ridden up the pass; that from the

---

OPPOSITE *A Persian miniature of 1573 showing the poet Firdausi with the court poets of Ghazni in a stylized landscape of cypress trees, flowering almonds and spring flowers.*

13

top of the pass you have seen a second plain, with a second barrier of mountains in the distance, a hundred miles away; that you know that beyond these mountains lies yet another plain, and another; and that for days, even weeks, you must ride with no shade, and the sun overhead, and nothing but the bleached bones of dead animals strewing the track. Then when you come to trees and running water, you will call it a garden. It will not be flowers and their garishness that your eyes crave for, but a green cavern full of shadows and pools where goldfish dart, and the sound of a little stream.

Some hint of the continuing comfort afforded by the shade of a single tree and the gurgle of water can still be experienced at every little wayside stop, where truck-drivers and travelling families cluster, seated in a circle on rugs, and picnicking in every available patch of noontime shade. For the average Muslim the physical hardships of the desert climate are not yet alleviated by the air-conditioning of our Western society, and for them nothing can equal the elixir of cool shade under a burning overhead sun.

Under such harsh conditions, little grows without water; but with the rush of melting mountain snows comes a transient greenness and a blinding burst of flower colour, as I witnessed in the Tehran valley. It is the essence of this fleeting spring joy which the paradise garden seeks to perpetuate throughout the whole year, which early miniature painters portrayed and about which poets wrote and still continue to write, setting their stories of traditional heroes and heroines within the flowering walls of a secret garden or hunting park.

The enclosed garden still exists throughout the Middle East for, unlike a European street where the proud gardener seeks to show off his horticultural expertise to the passing world, the emergent middle-class houseowner in the Middle East still surrounds his home with high walls, to create his personal paradise for himself and his family to enjoy in total privacy.

But beneath the superficial delights of the Middle Eastern garden lies a far deeper significance: in Islam no pleasure is taken at random; each is part of a greater unity; every individual aspect of the Truth links laterally with other aspects and can be analysed individually to discover its relevance within the whole. For tradition is all in Islam, and its basic truths and laws apply to every artistic aspect of man's endeavours, not least to his buildings, their form and layout, their structure and decoration.

It follows that, in such a harsh climate, the element of sanctuary which

OPPOSITE *A Mughal miniature of 1595 illustrating an incident when the owner of a garden discovers maidens bathing in his pool. The picture incorporates many of the elements of the ideal Islamic garden, with its pool (replete with maidens), canals and pavilion.*

the garden offers forms no insignificant part of the total concept; but it is the layout, the plan and the material from which it is conceived that are of interest, rather than the horticultural content.

Nevertheless, plants are loved passionately, for if nothing else they have a rarity value in certain parts of Islam, and they are of course an integral part of the garden. Certain trees, too, are used structurally in the design concept, but the idea of a landscaped garden, in which flowering objects and pattern are welded together to form a total entity, is foreign to this part of the world. In the gardens of Islam, individual plants seem to be positioned at random, often as a lovely but incidental feature. This is not to denigrate their value within the total concept for, time and again in Persian literature, analogies are drawn between the characteristics of certain plants and the character of man: we and they are all part of the same totality and subject to the same physical environment; and this concept of being physically rooted in solid matter and growing upwards and outwards is important. The plant/flower motif occurs again and again: in illustrations, in carpet patterns and in the arabesques of decoration.

It is this concept, the interlinking of the sentient animal, man, with the vegetable object, the garden, that has led to such a high degree of refinement in the Islamic garden, but a refinement which has not degenerated into dull uniformity, for the traditional and well-worn concept is allowed to develop with particular variations according to climate and locations.

This concept was based on pre-Islamic ideology, but its realization from the time of the Prophet proceeded right through early Persian culture, and wherever Islam extended its reach: into Sicily, southern Spain, along the coast of North Africa, Ottoman Turkey and back through Safavid Persia into the Mughal gardens of India, to reappear in nineteenth-century Qajar Persia again.

It is this extraordinarily strong tradition, based on the ethics of an equally strong civilization, that we seek to trace here. For gardens are the reflection of an essentially peaceful society – no matter how transitory that peace may be – and it would seem opportune to explain this tradition to the peoples of both the Middle East and the West, at a time when new tracts of it are entering daily into a technological age. But man does not change, even though the structure and shape of his buildings may; nor does the climate, or his religion, so surely the garden tradition should remain the same?

THE CONCEPT OF THE PARADISE GARDEN

The diversity of peoples, of temperature ranges and climates, of social conditions, and of those regions which Islam encompasses is enormous. A great concentration of its disciples lies in the Middle East, but it extends eastwards into India, South-East Asia, Malaysia and Indonesia and even into China. Northwards, it stretches from its holy centre at Mecca in Saudi Arabia through Iran, Turkey and what is now the southern Soviet Union. Southwards, Islam reaches into the heart of Africa, from where (until the fifteenth century) it reached through Spain into central France.

Islam, then, is not a single place or just a religion; it is a way of life for the vast numbers of people in those areas. The rules of Islam are set out in the Holy Book, the Quran. For the Muslim, this is the direct word of God as revealed to His Prophet Muhammad through the archangel Gabriel. This revelation took place at the beginning of the seventh century AD, and ended with the death of the Prophet in AD 632.

The Quran dictates how those of Islam should live their lives; it outlines a series of laws circumscribing what they may and may not do, and constantly draws similes and analogies to make its points more clear, very much in the way the Christian prophets told parables. The garden is constantly cited as a symbol for paradise, with shade and water as its ideal elements. 'Gardens underneath which rivers flow' is a frequently used expression for the bliss of the faithful, and occurs more than thirty times throughout the Quran. Four main rivers of paradise are also specified, one of water, one of milk, one of wine and one of purified honey. This

is the origin of the quartered garden, known in Persian as the *chahar bagh*, or four gardens, which were divided by means of four water-channels and all contained within a private, walled enclosure.

Also frequently mentioned are the abundant fruit trees in the paradise garden and the rich pavilions set among them, wherein the owners of the gardens and their friends might relax. Thus, within this concept of paradise is a clear indication as to what the garden should contain: fruit trees, water and rich pavilions, intended as places for pleasure and cool enjoyment. To a desert people, this concept was desirable as an ultimate perfection which contrasted sharply with the stark reality of the desert in which they lived. Descriptions of gardens in the Quran may have been inspired by the actual gardens of Damascus, a town which would have been seen and appreciated by merchants from Mecca at the end of their long caravan-route and which must have seemed a veritable paradise in contrast to the arid wilderness of their homeland.

Other civilizations, such as those of the ancient Egyptians or the Vikings, imagined paradise as a continuation of life on earth, but with none of its disadvantages. The early Muslims, however, living in one of the most inhospitable parts of the world, saw paradise as a complete contrast. After spreading out of the Arabian peninsula, they proceeded to create in their conquered lands the closest possible version of paradise on earth in superb gardens which spanned the Islamic world.

To the Muslim the beauty of the garden, and indeed of the whole of creation, was held to be a reflection of God. Some of the greatest out-pourings of Islamic poetry glorify this, and poets constantly used the image of the garden to describe their feelings towards a beloved. The great mystic Sufi poet Rumi used much garden imagery:

> The trees are engaged in ritual prayer and the birds in
> singing the litany,
> the violet is bent down in prostration.

or again

> See the upright position form the Syrian rose,
> and the violet the genuflection,
> the leaf has attained prostration: refresh the Call to Prayer!

OPPOSITE *In this Persian miniature of 1686 (from a book recounting the deeds of Ali – the Prophet's cousin and son-in-law – and his companions) paradise itself is illustrated as a* chahar bagh, *or quartered garden, resplendent with brightly coloured flowers.*

*The pattern and motifs of a Persian garden carpet, which here include
fish and deer as well as trees and plants,
reflect both the formal divisions and the content
of a* chahar bagh *or a paradise garden.*

So all-pervasive was this idea of the garden, that not only poets but all artists included references to gardens in their repertoire; not only were houses and palaces set in gardens, but their interiors glowed with representations of them, too – in mosaics, paintings and ceramics, and even on carpets. On these can be seen quite clearly the arrangement of the *chahar bagh*, with either an octagonal pool placed in it or perhaps a tomb or pavilion at its centre, or the great landscaped garden with pavilions providing a series of beautiful perspectives. A third type was to appear in India, where the form of the garden became that of a palace itself.

The Quran, therefore, is not, like the New Testament, a record of the prophet's activities and teachings on earth; it is believed to be the actual Word of God. So what it relates about the garden, its form and content, is not merely descriptive: God has actually defined paradise as a garden, and it is up to the individual not only to aspire to it in the after-life, but also to try to create its image here on earth. The way in which this Word of God was, and is, presented to man was also important, giving the Arabic script in which it was written far greater significance than that possessed by mere printed records of events. When you consider, too, that an early Islamic concept equated the depiction of a human image with idolatry, it is not hard to understand why the art of calligraphy should reach such a supremely high standard of artistic expression.

At another level, calligraphic pattern is used as pure decoration, together with abstract or geometric design, to cover, on the grandest scale, both the interior and exterior of a building, or on a much smaller scale to decorate a plate or vase. The mystical and universal equality of value which is placed on each element of a design, on whatever scale, establishes the unity of style which is so significant in all the artistic outpourings of Islam.

A similar totality of concept even applies to the location of a major building within a city, to its internal design and, more relevantly, to the spaces leading to it and those within as well. All aspects are locked together in a total cosmic plan, so that the user cannot be unaware of an ever-present God, both in him and about him in all the comings and goings of his daily life. Such an organization of mass and void, of spatial linkages, provides an orderly system for the individual that allows for both per-manency and change, for inward-looking privacy and for outward appreciation.

In opposition to the Western attitude and its concentration on the external look of a building, the traditional Islamic concern is primarily for the feel of space within, defined by its building materials. Volume is more important than mass, and then the quality of that volume, its light, its coolness and its decoration. The result is an internal architecture, inseparable from the fabric of the city, less concerned with buildings in space, more with space itself. Such a concept mirrors the ideal human condition: a lack of concern with outward symbols, but space for the inner soul to breathe and develop. To attain this inner peace within the teeming

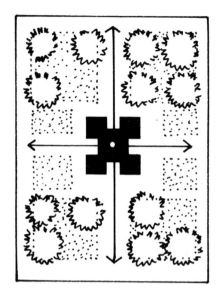

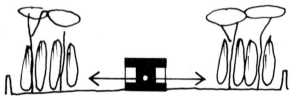

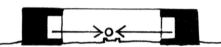

*The concept of the garden as a reflection of the cosmos. On the left
a centrifugal, or outward-directed, force flows out from the building
into a natural paradise; on the right a centripetal, or inner-directed,
force flows in to a fountain, which in turn generates ever-widening ripples,
so recommencing the cycle of expansion and contraction.*

streets and bazaars of a Middle Eastern township, a measure of personal
privacy has to be achieved, aided in public by a complete avoidance of
sensuous stimuli, for to keep quiet in a public place is to create one's own
sphere of privacy. The extreme example is that of the traditional Muslim
woman behind her veil, which externally creates a walled space of infinite
privacy. The close packing of residential units, each with its own courtyard
garden and surrounding walls, is the urban family's manifestation of this
sense of place.

The converse form, exhibiting an outward-directed, or centrifugal, force,
is found in the *chahar bagh*, or quartered garden, in which a central pavilion

is sited at the intersection of four avenues, typified in the Hasht Behist of Isfahan (literally, eight paradises). Here is a truly dynamic paradise, not only in the overall plan, but in the very concept of its central pavilion. For the pavilion provides a primary centrifugal movement outwards along the avenues and a secondary inward-directed motion through its four porches to the basin of water and the fountain – its spiritual centre – from which in turn are generated ripples of ever-expanding diameter, recommencing the cycle of expansion and contraction.

The larger, centrifugal type of garden was not feasible within limited city space, so the courtyard plan is the more acceptable urban form of garden which is still capable of providing that contact with nature so highly valued by its inhabitants. The form of urban dwelling surrounding an internal courtyard, which was anticipated by the typical Roman town house and well-suited to a hot climate, became the prototype for architectural forms and is repeated in mosque, madrasa (college) and caravanserai.

The enclosed garden thus also becomes a defined space, encompassing within itself a total reflection of the cosmos and, hence, paradise. Within it, this concept fosters order and harmony, and can be manifested to the senses through numbers, geometry, colour and, of course, materials. But the interaction of these elements of shape and space must create a place that is totally restful, devoid of tensions and conducive to contemplation. Within this space, the traditional pool provides a centre and an upward-reflecting surface for directing the creative imagination.

In a climate of long summer heat, much of day-to-day living takes place out of doors, so the transitional area from the building to the world outside is important for it provides the link. (In the Alhambra the device is used to such an extent that the visitor is never sure whether he is inside or out.) It was this transitional space that inevitably became the reception area in palace buildings, for inside was private and outside was for quiet contemplation. Known in Iran as the *talar*, this porch-like structure provides the link, keeping the sun off those under its roof and shading the structure it adjoins. It appears in all traditional buildings and reappears in various modern structural forms. While the *talar* is static, in a directional form it becomes the colonnade.

Metaphysically, the *talar* is viewed as the locus of the soul moving between garden and building, where garden is spirit and building body.

ABOVE *A* talar, *or porch, at Mahan in Iran with a decorative*
band of Kufic script along the top.
The talar *provides a transitional space between*
the interior and the exterior, which is significant
on both a physical and a spiritual level.

It is therefore the transitional space between the spiritual and terrestrial worlds. Another form of the *talar*, this time arched, is known as the *ivan*; it occurs in mosque layout, though as an architectural structure it had also been used in pre-Islamic buildings.

The metaphysics of Islamic thought and its application to the concept of traditional architectural elements are the bond linking Isfahan, Granada and Agra. They may differ in structure, scale, age and usage – in everything, in fact, but their common denominator: that they were built by Muslims for Muslim usage. However, this single factor transcends all other structural differences and it is this which unifies all the regions of Islam.

OPPOSITE *An* ivan, *or portal, of the Royal Mosque in Isfahan, Iran.*
Like the talar, *the* ivan *provides a transitional space*
but is normally applied to larger buildings like mosques.

GARDEN ORIGINS

We have considered the meaning and the importance of the garden within Islam but this mystical paradise must have had some precedent. After all, the garden is used as a symbol in many religions, for example the Garden of Eden. Beyond this, the obvious sense of stability to be gained from the possession of a garden must also have been generally recognized as being important to a migratory tribal community in Arabia. While religions might change, the hard climate of the Middle East and the need for water and coolness had not, hence its valued use as simile in the Quran. Actual gardens, however, must have been scarce, thereby adding to their aesthetic value, although it is difficult to know just when an enclosure round, say, an oasis becomes a garden. One suspects that, to the desert nomad, a few trees to provide shade do become just that. As long as shade and water are abundant, an Eastern garden need contain very little of merit in the way of plants to be imbued with endless qualities of relaxation and physical enjoyment. Persian poets may have praised what, to our botanically attuned senses, would seem disappointingly little. And this probably holds good for early Western gardens as well, where time and the land for decorative garden treatment were at a premium.

Persia was one of the first states to be conquered by the newly emerging force of Islam, after the reigning Sassanian dynasty was defeated in battle in AD 642. For over a thousand years the Persian Empire had been a major power in Western Asia and many Arabians had been vassals of Persian rulers. Islam burst upon Persia with the speed of a desert whirlwind

OPPOSITE ABOVE *The expansion of Islam up to AD 750.*

OPPOSITE BELOW *The extent of Islam c. 1650.*

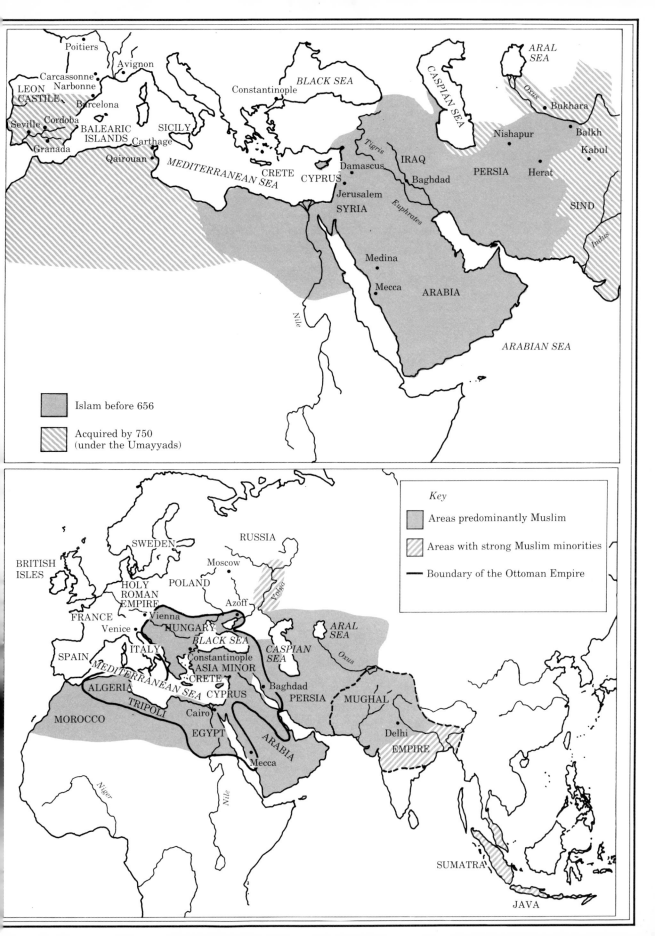

Map 1 (top):

Poitiers

Avignon

Carcassonne
Narbonne

LEON
CASTILE

Barcelona

Seville · Cordoba

BALEARIC
ISLANDS

Granada

Carthage

Qairouan

BLACK SEA

Constantinople

CASPIAN SEA

ARAL SEA

Oxus

Bukhara

Nishapur

Balkh

Kabul

SICILY

MEDITERRANEAN SEA

CRETE SEA

CYPRUS

Damascus

IRAQ

Tigris

Baghdad

PERSIA

Herat

SIND

Indus

Jerusalem

SYRIA

Euphrates

Nile

Medina

Mecca

ARABIA

ARABIAN SEA

Islam before 656

Acquired by 750
(under the Umayyads)

Map 2 (bottom):

Key

Areas predominantly Muslim

Areas with strong Muslim minorities

Boundary of the Ottoman Empire

SWEDEN

RUSSIA

BRITISH
ISLES

Moscow

POLAND

Volga

ARAL SEA

HOLY
ROMAN
EMPIRE

Vienna

Azoff

Oxus

FRANCE

HUNGARY

Venice

BLACK SEA

CASPIAN SEA

SPAIN

ITALY

Constantinople

ASIA MINOR

CRETE

CYPRUS

Baghdad

PERSIA

MUGHAL

MEDITERRANEAN SEA

ALGERIA

TRIPOLI

Cairo

Delhi

MOROCCO

EGYPT

EMPIRE

Niger

ARABIA

Nile

Mecca

SUMATRA

JAVA

and quickly superseded its preceding religion of Zoroastrianism, which venerated fire as a manifestation of the divine. Persian life and its architectural endeavours continued, however, as Islam had so far no tradition with which to replace them. Thus, the new philosophy grafted itself onto an older stable civilization in which the garden held an undoubted and established part. One of the strengths of Islam lay in this continued assimilation of other established civilizations as it raced its course round the Mediterranean during the next hundred years, and then the cross-fertilization of each within the Islamic empire.

It is in early Persian origins, then, that we must seek the garden's source. But it is relevant at this stage to look at how water is used in Iran to irrigate land and to see how a pattern evolved which later became formalized, taking on other significances. It is a tradition which has probably not changed in thousands of years, and builders of early palaces would have regularized and expanded the same methods to achieve some of the grandiose water layouts which we know existed in conjunction with early palace buildings, for garden and building were always inseparable.

The mountain has been venerated in the Middle East since the earliest times, and some of the earliest buildings were of ziggurat formation (the hanging Gardens of Babylon, for instance), which was a ritual imitation of familiar sacred mountains surrounding the Iranian plateau. One of the reasons for venerating the mountain may have been that from it flows life-giving water in this desert landscape when, with melting snows in spring, thousands of rushing streams flow downwards. Their lifetime is short, however, and few streams and fewer rivers ever reach the sea, as they die out very quickly in the heat of the desert. Even the famed river Zayandeh, by which Isfahan stands and which is so beautifully bridged, disappears into a salt lake only a few miles further on.

But where water failed, man as early as the sixth century BC started to dig subterranean water channels (known in Persia as *qanats*) to lead the water from the mountain to the villages and fields. *Qanats* are constructed by digging a shaft to pierce the permanent raised water table situated at the foot of the mountain. This level is still above that of the eventual water delivery point, from where an underground channel is excavated back to the base of the main shaft slightly uphill. The length of the *qanat* may be either only a few metres or up to several kilometres, and the course is punctuated by vertical shafts every fifty metres or so, both to provide

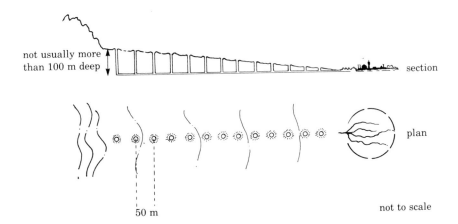

not usually more
than 100 m deep

section

plan

50 m

not to scale

TOP *Plan and section of the construction of a typical* qanat.
*Water is collected from under the foothills of a mountain range and
conducted by qanats, or underground channels, to its destination, which
is often at some considerable distance from the source.
Vertical shafts provide air and access for the diggers.*

ABOVE Qanat *holes punctuate the central Iranian desert landscape.*

an air supply to the diggers and to bring up the excavated material. The lines of these mini-craters are a typical feature traversing the Iranian desert. Some distance from the eventual delivery point, the *qanat* becomes an open water channel, often closely planted on either side with chenars. Upon emerging, the water is first claimed by the owner of the *qanat* or his lessee for his own use, and from his collecting tank it may then flow perhaps through a water-mill, before being used in the village and then out into the fields for irrigation, where it divides into grid patterns.

It is from the stylization of these grid patterns, between which crops or fruit trees and eventually flowers were planted, that the typical early garden layout developed. The catchment pool became a feature in the layout and was treated in ever more decorative ways. The grid network, under Islam, was characteristically reorganized into extended geometric patterns, suggesting boundlessness and infinite divisibility, while planting within the compartments complemented and balanced the whole conception which was viewed as a recapitulation of paradise. Pools within the pattern became main features, always brimming with water, for Persian pools are raised above ground level, with the pressure of the downward-flowing stream forcing their overflow over the raised sides of the pool to a surrounding trough at ground level, from which the water flows on. The pool as such reflects heaven in its shimmering surface, thus uniting the exalted with the mundane in a symbolism central to Islamic perspective. Later developments produced descending pools with rushing water between them and ultimately pressure-raised fountains spouting through metal nozzles, spraying and cooling the air.

A lesser water engineering feat, which there is no reason to suppose has changed in a thousand years, is the catchment of water laterally from a main fast-descending stream. It is then transported in man-made channels, either dug or constructed with brushwood and mud at a slower level of descent, irrigating as it flows, and eventually ends in a catchment tank, which is used as a reservoir when the stream ultimately fails in summer.

PERSIA

The earliest form of garden or park which we know of in Persia dates approximately from the sixth century BC and surrounded the palace of Pasargadae built by the Achaemenid, Cyrus the Great. This in itself was a series of buildings or pavilions within a walled enclosure of considerable area, which had little in common with the later European concept of a single large building containing the entire court structure. Such a form was also typical of the nomadic way of life with its multiplicity of occupation space where no distinction was made between eating, sleeping and living areas; distinctions between the various rooms and buildings were for climatic rather than utilitarian reasons, and movement on the domestic level was from winter to summer rooms rather than from eating to sleeping areas. At a regal level, movement was from palace to palace, hence the construction of Pasargadae and Susa in the south and Ecbatana (Hamadan) in the north.

Although Pasargadae is now in ruins, it is situated in a beautiful, silent

*Plan of the palace of Pasargadae, near Isfahan, Iran,
built by Cyrus the Great in the sixth century BC.
Wide* talar *porches supported by columns surrounded all the buildings.*

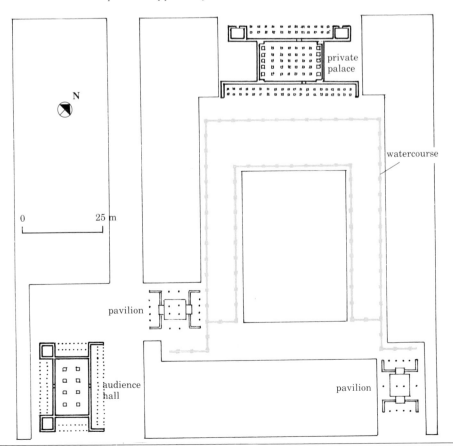

expanse of parklike meadow in which were sited two palaces, two pavilions and a linking stone watercourse with pools at regular intervals, which quite clearly was part of a formal garden and probably acted as an irrigational channel as well. Each of the pavilions looking towards the watercourse has an extensive colonnade which is considerably larger than the building behind it: this would indicate that they were for viewing the garden from the shade, the forerunner of the *talar* or columned porch in fact. This aspect of the garden, to be viewed rather than used, was a constant factor in Persian layout and was commented on by the traveller Sir John Chardin in the seventeenth century who wrote that: 'The Persians don't walk so much in gardens as we do, but content themselves with a bare Prospect; and breathing the fresh Air; For this End, they set themselves down in some part of the Garden, at their first coming into it, and never move from their Seats till they are going out of it.' (*Voyage de Paris à Isfahan*, 1723.)

We know a considerable amount about the palace of Susa: what it was made of, where it came from and that it surrounded a courtyard; however, we have even greater detail of the building at Persepolis from Cyrus' successor, Darius himself. Within the complex there were areas of gardenry and it was surrounded by sumptuous gardens and palaces, for the monarchy occupied the palace itself only for ceremonial – not living – purposes.

But within our context, the real interest lies in both the extensive sources of the building materials and the diversity of origins of the slave labour used: Assyrians, Egyptians, Babylonians, Ethiopians, Sardians, Medes, Ionians – for this would indicate the vast range of outside influences which had always played such a great part in the Persian ethos. Persia had always been one of the mercantile crossroads of the ancient world: of silk routes over the Oxus to China, of spice routes from India and salt routes from Arabia; and Darius must also have been influenced by Egyptian culture dating from his offensive there. Certainly the influence of Egyptian architecture is strong within Persepolis, although the total conception is far more lucid and humane than a pure Egyptian building.

The conclusion to be drawn is of the amazing cultural cross-fertilization which must have affected this part of the world, even before Alexander the Great caused the fall of Persepolis, bringing Greek and, later, Roman concepts as well.

For the chronology of subsequent early buildings and their surroundings

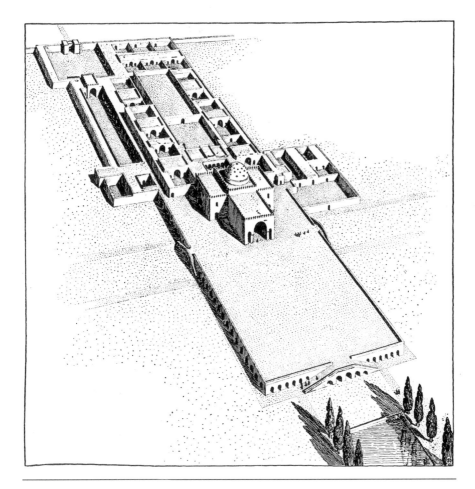

up to the end of Sassanian times (AD 642), one can do no better than quote the findings of the art historian Ralph Pinder-Wilson, who has researched the Imarat-i Khusraw at Qasr-i Shirin, on the road to Kirmanshah. This building of Khusraw II Parviz (AD 591–628) stood on a high terrace and, according to Arab historians, was in the centre of a great paradise garden or park, containing rare animals and surrounded by a wall. Another wall within this enclosed the palace and the inner garden. The nature of this garden is unknown but he infers, from the traces of a great pool which lay

ABOVE *Reconstruction of the Imarat-i Khusraw at Qasr-i Shirin in Iran, showing the beginning of the great pool and the arched openings of the passageway beneath the terrace. The palace was built for Khusraw II between AD 591 and 628 and was encircled by a large park.*

between the palace and the monumental entrance portal set in the east side of the enclosing wall, that it comprised vistas. At the garden level, a vaulted passageway runs around the three sides of the eastern half of the terrace. The outer wall of this passageway is pierced by round-headed arches at regular intervals, with vaulted chambers cut into the terrace on the inner side of the passageway. It seems highly probable that these deep-vaulted arcades were intended to provide a cool retreat from the intense summer heat similar to the colonnaded porticos of Pasargadae.

Pinder-Wilson goes on to explain that not far from the Imarat-i Khusraw is a smaller palace of the same period called Hawsh-Kuri, also with vaulted chambers serving the same purpose. An avenue ran from the eastern side of the palace to a pavilion, suggesting that here too was a garden. Yet another avenue led from the north-east corner of the palace to the monumental portal of an enclosed garden, measuring 670 × 600 metres. The upper room of the entrance portal offers a wide view of the park enclosure and anticipates later pavilions with commanding prospects.

Thus, already established is the typical relationship between the pavilion or palace and a formal garden which required an ornamental pool or canal, being decorative as well as irrigational. Pinder-Wilson goes on to say that the incorporation of Mesopotamia with Persia into the Islamic world allowed the concept of the Persian garden to travel to Syria, Egypt and the Maghrib, or western empire, and Persia assumed the dominant role in the artistic as well as the political life of Islam.

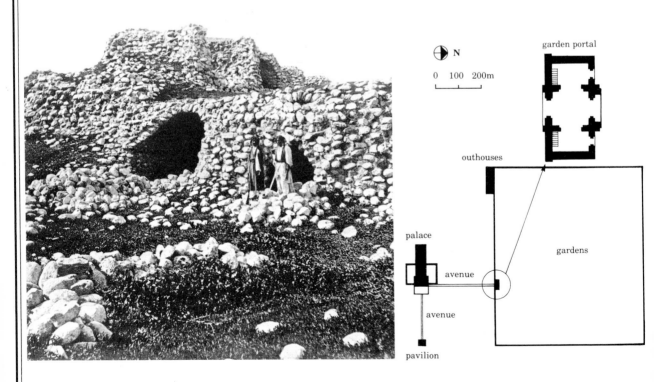

garden portal

N

0   100   200m

outhouses

palace

avenue

gardens

avenue

pavilion

Under Islamic rule, Arab leaders were known as khalifs. The word 'khalif' derives from an Arabic word meaning successor, since the khalifs succeeded Muhammad in his role as head of the Muslim community. The first khalifs, the Umayyads (AD 661–750), were displaced by the Abbasid khalifs, who founded a new city at Baghdad. Here, Persian Sassanian architecture replaced that of Hellenistic Syria, where the dispossessed Umayyad khalifs had had their capital. Little remains of the Abbasids in Baghdad, but in Samarra, which temporarily replaced it as the capital from AD 838 to 892, the ruins of a whole city still exist. Inside the city stood Jawsaq al-Khaqani, the palace built by the khalif al-Mutasim. Within the palace a complex of gardens appears for the first time in an urban context: and within one of the courtyards of Jawsaq al-Khaqani was a great canal or pool similar to that of the Imarat-i Khusraw but without the surrounding gardens. Instead, the Abbasid khalifs had to be content with inner courts planted with flowers. In the densely populated cities of Baghdad and Samarra houses had their own gardens, which were presumably decorative since fruit and cereals were cultivated outside the city walls. At Samarra, after the city was laid out on the east bank of the river Tigris, a bridge was built leading to market gardens and orchards on the west bank, which were irrigated by canals dug from the Tigris. A very early Muslim example of the *chahar bagh* concept is also to be found at Samarra: the Bulkawara Palace, built between AD 849 and 859, was approached through a succession of three courts, all quartered by inter-secting paths or watercourses, and at the other end there was a quadri-partite garden, flanked by pavilions overlooking the river. This, according to John D. Hoag in *Western Islamic Architecture*, was 'probably an intentional evocation of the Quran's paradise'.

In the following (tenth) century when western Persia became independent under the family of the Buyids, they chose Shiraz as their capital. There is a contemporary account of a two-storeyed palace there, around which were laid out orchards and groves. Streams were introduced into the palace for coolness, and they flowed through the rooms and arcaded courts, implying a close connection between the indoors and the out-of-doors. These are illustrated by later Persian miniature painters.

With the advent of the Saljuqs (1038–1194), the word *bagh* (Persian for garden) starts to be used to denote an entity comprising both palace or pavilions and garden, much as the word 'villa' covers both in the Renaiss-

OPPOSITE LEFT *The remains of vaulted chambers at the palace of Hawsh Kuri.*

OPPOSITE RIGHT *The plan of the palace of Hawsh Kuri, which was situated a short distance from the Imarat-i Khusraw, Iran, and built in the same period, displays a strong linear form in the general layout of avenues, pavilions and a large enclosed garden.*

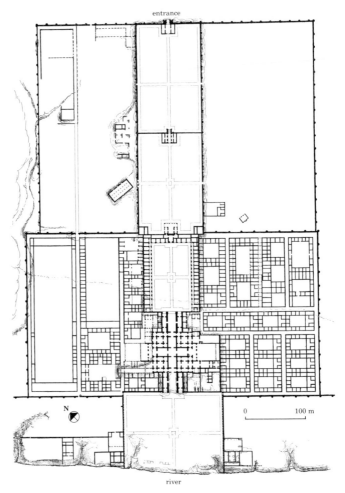

entrance

N

0   100 m

river

*Plan of the Bulkawara Palace at Samarra, Iraq, built between AD 849
and 859, showing the quadripartite courts and gardens, which are among
the earliest examples of the Islamic chahar bagh concept.*

ance Italian layouts. Thus, by this time the main forms of the Persian
garden had developed, integrating the paradise or hunting park of the
Achaemenids with the *bagh* or smaller decorative garden area, sometimes
within the paradise garden. The Quran, however, does not define which
form of garden it means when it describes paradise. It is the development
of the *bagh* that we shall follow, but next in the south of Spain, since it is
there that some of the earliest gardens in this tradition still exist.

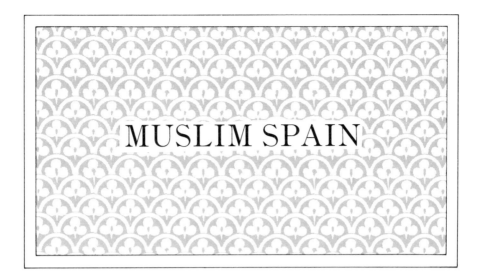

MUSLIM SPAIN

Spain was first attacked by Muslim raiders as early as AD 710, when Berber tribesmen from North Africa landed on the Andalusian coast. The following year, another attack was mounted and a foothold was gained within an already weakened country, upset by feuding native Visigothic princes. An easy advance was made over the whole peninsula, with the exception of the mountainous area on the south shore of the Bay of Biscay. By 719 Carcassonne and Narbonne in France were taken, then Avignon and Poitiers fell in 732, but this marked the limits of the Muslim advance before they were engaged in battle. Their defeat there broadly marks the time of their retreat into Spain, although there was a Muslim presence in France for some time. This western outpost of Islam was consolidated at this time under the Umayyad khalifate, ruled until the Abbasid seizure of power from Damascus in Syria. After their displacement by the Abbasids, the Umayyads withdrew to Spain and eventually established their own khalifate there in 912. Muslim Spain was known as al-Andalus (although the area which we know as Andalusia is now only a small southern part of it). Cordoba became its capital, with Toledo and Seville and, later, Granada as major cities of art and culture. Being located in the south, these cities were in easy communication with North Africa.

While Islamic fervour was as strong in al-Andalus as in Baghdad, the Spanish Umayyads were a constant source of defiance to the Abbasid khalifs of Baghdad and, later, the Egyptian Fatimid khalifs. Pride in their Arab origins inspired them to make al-Andalus a realm in which Arab culture remained more vigorous than in the east, where Persian and then Turkish influence was becoming increasingly dominant. Islam in Spain overlaid a previous Christian civilization and, earlier still, a Roman culture, with, later, strong Jewish overtones as well. Rŏman irrigation systems were still in use when the Arabs arrived in 711. In its usual way Islam absorbed these separate cultures to produce a refined society with no contemporary parallels in Europe, and very few since.

CORDOBA

We gather from al-Idrisi, one of the greatest geographers of the Middle Ages, that Cordoba was a city made up of five continuous smaller cities which covered a distance of 5 kilometres from east to west. The bridge over the river Guadalquivir, or Wadi al-Kabir as the Arabs would have known it, surpassed all others for its beauty and solidity, with its seventeen arches. The environs of the city covered a distance of 32 kilometres the greater part taken up by gardens of various palaces and mosques. Both these and the surrounding fertile plain were fed by an irrigational system from great subterranean reservoirs and a matrix of small canals which would again dictate the form of subsequent gardens.

Neglected after the repulsion of the Muslim invaders, the land surrounding Cordoba eventually returned to its original aridity. It is about these once rich lands of the Sierra of Cordoba that a story is told of the poet king, al-Mutamid of Seville. Born in 1040, al-Mutamid, like his predecessors, was passionately fond of flowers and gardens. Once, his wife Rumaykiyya, noted for her skill and wit in verse, was in the palace watching snow falling, when she burst into tears. Her husband, she declared, must provide this lovely sight each winter or take her to a land where it snows every winter. The king promised to grant her wish: 'Thou shalt have snow each winter even here; such is my word.' He promptly ordered the Sierra of Cordoba to be planted with almond trees, so that after the frosts of winter the bare brown hills were clothed for Rumaykiyya's delight in delicate pink snow.

The fulcrum of this urbane and hedonistic society was the Great Mosque,

OPPOSITE *The Great Mosque, or Mezquita, at Cordoba with the cathedral of Charles V breaking out of the middle of it and the tenth-century Patio de los Naranjos in the foreground. The naves of the mosque, now closed, were open to the courtyard and their lines are continued by the rows of orange trees.*

so huge that even today the cathedral erected in its midst by Charles V is still engulfed by it. It has been said that the mosque originally extended over the site of a Visigothic church, and both Christians and Muslims shared the area, which was some indication of the tolerance shown by Islam at the time! Eventually the Christians were given a site for their own cathedral on the outskirts of the town when the mosque was built by Abd al-Rahman I. His heir added galleries for women and a fountain for ablutions with a minaret in the external courtyard.

The mosque was later expanded by Abd al-Rahman II from a previous low building, similar to the mosques of tenth-century Syria, and consisted of nineteen naves of pillars in a double arcade, possibly inspired by the structure of Roman aqueducts, many of the columns being used from the previously existing building, together with Roman pillars. The naves, though now closed, were open to the courtyard, and their forest-like pattern of pillars is repeated in rows of orange trees planted across the courtyard, which in turn are regimented by formalized irrigation canals. The courtyard, known as the Patio de los Naranjos (Court of the Orange Trees), was claimed by Mrs C. Villiers-Stuart, author of *Spanish Gardens*, to be the oldest existing garden in Europe, and represented an early urbanization of the standard Middle Eastern concept of planting fruit

Stone-edged canals, which channel water to the orange trees, emphasize the regular pattern of the Patio de los Naranjos. The original Muslim fountains were replaced by Renaissance substitutes.

trees within a grid plan. Supposedly laid out by Hisham II's despotic chamberlain, al-Mansur, in AD 976, the area is rectangular approximately 60 × 130 metres with the planting divided into three plots, each with a fountain in the centre, and the customary palm marking each corner of the design. Water from the fountains fills the stone-edged irrigation canals that feed the trees, and it is this need for irrigation which must have kept the plan intact.

The first Umayyads lived in Cordoba itself in a palace called al-Rusafa, named after one outside Damascus built by the grandfather of Abd al-Rahman I, where he had been brought up. He introduced to the garden of the palace many rare and exotic plants, his agents seeking them as far afield as Syria, Turkestan and even India. Among them were the date palm and the pomegranate, both introductions to Spain, the latter now being the emblem (if not the source of the name) of Granada. Later, to fit his new eminence as the khalif as well as emir, and taking the throne under the name of al-Nasir li-Din Allah, Abd al-Rahman III decided to construct a palace city for his household three miles to the west of Cordoba on a long slope of the Sierra Morena, a site which, though less defensible than the Alhambra (which we know was then a citadel in Granada) was nevertheless four times larger. This was called Madinat al-Zahra, after the khalif's favourite wife. Work began around AD 936 and continued for about forty years, but was destroyed within fifty years by the Berbers.

After Pasargadae in faraway Persia, the palace of Madinat al-Zahra with its surrounding gardens is the most important early secular construction in this chronology, for it still exists in part, and is currently undergoing extensive restoration. But from where did the inspiration for such a palace come? The Sassanian palace of Imarat-i Khusraw at Qasr-i Shirin, standing in its hunting park on a terrace, must have been known, as must the Abbasid palace of Jawsaq al-Khaqani at Samarra. There must also have been some rumour of the Buyid gardens of early Shiraz, laid out with orchards and groves and with streams of coolness running through arcaded courtyards and palace rooms. Egypt too must have contributed, as it is said that from the legendary richness of the Fatimid courts, themselves influenced by Persian and Byzantine splendour, there came the idea of using quicksilver, which was plentiful in Spain. Al-Nasir purportedly used it to fill the central pool of a hall in which he received ambassadors. It is said that the walls of the room were of marble inlaid with gold, and on each side eight doors of ebony and gold were set between piers of coloured marble and crystal. While the khalif entertained – perhaps displaying the room's chief ornament, a huge pearl presented by Leo, ruler of Byzantium – he would signal a slave to disturb the pool, at which all the walls of the room became a kaleidoscope of reflected colour, dazzling the kings of Leon and Navarre when they sought an audience, and even impressing the emperor's ambassadors from Constantinople. Other influences would have affected the design, layout and decoration of Madinat al-Zahra too: workmen from Byzantine Constantinople, who had recently completed the great mosque, were said to have built the central pavilion. It was no wonder that word of the luxuries of Madinat al-Zahra echoed round the Mediterranean.

The complex of buildings consisted of three terraces. The upper one contained the main palace buildings, the khalif's reception rooms, his residence and harem, which alone was said to house 6,300. According to Arab historians, the palace contained 4,300 pillars and 500 decorated doorways. Those pillars that did not come from Roman ruins in Spain or North Africa were imported by sea from Italy, France and the Byzantine empire, or fashioned from the quarries of al-Andalus. Al-Nasir kept up good relations with the Byzantine emperor at Constantinople to counterbalance the threat posed by his Islamic rivals.

Despite the oft-cited Muslim distaste for figurative representation, two famous fountains in the palace owed their beauty to the sculptor's art: one, a gilt bronze with reliefs of human figures, had come from Byzantine Constantinople; the other, of green marble, had come from Syria and was surrounded in its patio by figures of lions, crocodiles and deer. These figures made in al-Andalus were inlaid with gems and spouted water from their mouths. This sumptuous palace, conceived within a garden scheme and designed by architects from the eastern Islamic empire, anticipated Shah Jahan's luxurious court of the Red Fort at Delhi by several centuries. The two gardens are identical in conception and scale but are on different levels. They are both tripartite, although at Madinat al-Zahra the buildings interrupt.

The main room of Madinat al-Zahra faces an immense tank of water, to reflect the rich architecture of the hall. Palace and pool take up the northern half of the vertical axis. The intersection of the axes is marked by a large pavilion whose north side was reflected in the same pool, while its west, south and east sides were reflected in smaller pools, from which the respective halves of the horizontal and vertical axes set out. Irrigation was by narrow channels fed by the pools, running along both sides of each path with outlets (which have been uncovered intact) at a corner of a flower bed, to permit irrigation. The terrace level below this main pool repeats the plan of the first, with the exception of the buildings. The only difference discovered is a broad platform in the middle of the southern half of the vertical axis. It is supposed that this level contained a botanical garden with plants from other Muslim countries and a small game park. The early layout of Madinat al-Zahra owed much of its inspiration to the east: to Baghdad, to Damascus, to Hellenized Byzantium.

The central theme invariably common to them all is the use of water. In a garden, water is used as a central theme whether it be in pond, pool or basin, with or without a fountain. Running from the pool are paths

OPPOSITE BELOW *The view from inside the main hall at Madinat al-Zahra over a large tank of water to the central pavilion and gardens beyond.*

ABOVE *The remains of the tenth-century palace of Madinat al-Zahra, near Cordoba, reveal the formal layout of garden and pavilions. The main Hall of Audience on the left overlooks the foundations of the central pavilion, flanked by water tanks, on the right.*

dividing the garden into four. This type of quartered or quadripartite garden, in which the beds are often lower than the paths to facilitate irrigation, is seen again and again and it becomes the skeleton of the typical Moorish layout. It is similar in plan to the Persian ideal of the *chahar bagh* (four gardens) and the Mughal quartered garden of India, but smaller and more intimate in scale. It is this scheme, evident on a larger scale at Madinat al-Zahra, which links its tenth-century layout to the culmination of the Moorish garden-plan in the fourteenth-century Alhambra complex in Granada.

SEVILLE

Gardens of the eleventh century are more difficult to trace: indeed we are lucky to find any original Moorish building, let alone gardens, since succeeding Christian kings in Spain tried so hard to wipe out any evidence of infidel incursion into Spain. However, traces of a garden were found in a courtyard at the Aljaferia (al-Zafaryyah) of Zaragoza with a central axis and pool at either end, but no transversal axis, or any evidence of how the beds were irrigated. Fragments of two other gardens have been found in the Alcazar of Seville. As this complex stands today, dreamily romantic, it was laid out in 1364 for Pedro the Cruel, the King of Castile, by Moorish craftsmen who had been allowed to remain ('Glory to our Lord the Sultan Don Pedro', as one Arabic inscription there says), but this building was on the ruins of a formerly Moorish one. It is said that the patio of al-Mutamid's famous palace in Seville, the Qasr al-Mubarak, was covered by a twelfth-century quadripartite garden. All that is now visible are three sunken flower beds, and at each end of the central one there was probably a pool. The sides of the flower beds were stuccoed and painted, and they must have furnished the colour that was otherwise lacking in the winter season.

Elsewhere in the Alcazar, one side of an eleventh-century garden has come to light, also quadripartite but with flower beds sunk about five metres below the surrounding level; such was the elevation of the axes that they were really bridges supported by arches. The side walls are

OPPOSITE *The gardens of the Alcazar in Seville were laid out by Moorish craftsmen in 1364 for the Christian King of Castile. From a pool in the shape of the star of Islam a tile-lined channel leads down a walk flanked by clipped cypresses.*

composed of blind arches with clay water-pipes embedded in the brickwork of the arches. These particulars are enough to identify the garden described by Rodrigo Caro in the seventeenth century, before the garden was obliterated by earthquake tremors. He says:

from here one enters another courtyard known as Crucero, because it is cruciform in plan, and although one enters it on the same level as the previous area, below it lies a subterranean garden of orange trees, divided into four quarters; and it is so deep, in relation to the courtyard, that the tops of the trees almost reach the level of the paths. This rests on very powerful arches of brick and stone, with buttresses on either side, and they enclose a great pool of water which corresponds in shape to the cross above. Along the sides of this garden run corridors which support the paths; likewise there are corridors in the court above, which is all most beautifully worked with balustrades on either side, dressed with tilework. The water issues by fountain jet from a marble basin, which is surrounded by beautifully proportioned slabs of white marble. Thus this courtyard with the expanse of sky visible from it, its extraordinary scale and vistas in the subterranean garden, is very cheerful and grandiose and with the shade in its lower part is, during the summer, the shadiest and coolest of places. All this I believe to be a survival of the ancient Alcazar of the Moors ...

A twelfth-century garden in the Alcazar of Seville in the process of restoration.
It is conventionally quadripartite but has an unusual circular intersection
of the axes. The flower beds are sunk almost two metres below path level
and the original effect must have been like walking through a living carpet.

Another twelfth-century garden covering one of the earlier ones has been found practically intact and is being restored carefully; the plants originally grown in it have been identified, their pollen having lain there for eight centuries. The garden is the conventional quadripartite type, with, unique in Muslim Spain, a circular intersection of the axes, and a fountain in the middle whose sides were also painted. The flower beds were sunk deep, about two metres, and the side walls of the beds were composed of blind arches made in brick. Although both axes have watercourses down the middle of the path, no outlets that might explain how the beds were irrigated could be found, and irrigation was probably by hand.

GRANADA

A brief account of Muslim history and culture in Spain is necessary to link the tenth-century Umayyad rule in Cordoba to the thirteenth-century Nasrid rule in Granada. With the decline of Umayyad hegemony in the early eleventh century, al-Andalus was ruled from 1009 to 1091 by the Taifa kings – a collection of minor kings representing a *taifa*, or faction, each greedy for the other's territory. The feuding of these small states offered an opportunity to the Christian kings in the north, previously as divided as the Muslims, to unite in the prospect of reconquest. This they did, retaking Toledo in 1085.

North Africa, until recently a dependency of al-Andalus, had now become the empire of a Sahara-based dynasty (the forebears of the modern Tuaregs), who ruled the Meditteranean coast from Morocco to Western Algeria and were known as the Almoravids (from the Arabic *al-murabit*, 'those who live in religious retreats'). They exemplified the Berber devotion to Islam, although once in possession of al-Andalus, to which they came as rescuers and stayed as masters, they were quickly corrupted by the temptations offered by its hedonistic society.

After half a century and renewed anarchy, al-Andalus was again rescued by a second wave from North Africa in 1147, known as the Almohads – meaning 'the asserters of the unity of God'. They also were Berbers, but from the High Atlas mountains, not the desert. Their founder, Ibn Tumart, was a theologian of some sophistication, having previously studied in Cordoba as well as Alexandria, Mecca and Baghdad. Five Almohads ruled until the last, without an heir, delivered what was left by then of Muslim Spain into the hands of the Christians, with the exception of the last small kingdom of Granada, which became a Christian vassal state, miraculously surviving until 1492.

Two centuries divide the Christian reconquests in al-Andalus: the first was that of the Cordoban kaliphate in 1031, the second the capture of Seville in 1248, isolating Granada as a tiny sultanate containing one fertile valley, the Vega, and a chain of sea ports running round to Cadiz. This very isolation marks a turning point in the history of Granada, for in 1238 a feudal prince, Muhammad ibn Yusuf ibn Nasr, known as Ibn al-Ahmar, took the city and through his diplomacy and acceptance of Castilian suzerainty maintained himself not merely in Granada, but as the sole ruler of what was left of Muslim Spain. His twenty-two descendants of the Nasrid dynasty, as they were called, ruled until the final Christian conquest.

During these disruptive years in Spain, al-Andalus threw up men of towering intellect, scientists, philosophers, poets and mathematicians, all of whom were known and acknowledged throughout the Islamic world and whose thoughts and writings very much influenced later European thought. Despite the general winding down of the organized political and military state during the last period of Muslim rule in Spain, this strikingly rich and original culture was still evolving. This was based, firstly, on an economic prosperity culled from well-organized agriculture, built up over succeeding generations; and secondly, on the intensity of Islam, which increased as the state became the sanctuary for those of the faith who had been displaced by the Christian incursions elsewhere. This effect of concentration heightened Muslim awareness of their own tradition and history. It is within this historical and cultural setting that one has to consider the building of the Alhambra.

As early as the ninth century, a citadel existed there, known as al-Qalah al-Hamra or the 'Red Citadel'. The building is of brick made of ferrous mud which really does look red in the early-morning and late-evening sun. But it was not until Nasrid rule that the Alhambra became a city in itself, incorporating a royal palace.

According to the art historian Oleg Grabar, author of *The Alhambra*, we know that the gardens and pavilions of the Generalife date from the reign of Ismail (1315–25), but the most important remains of the Alhambra itself, the complexes of the Courts of the Myrtles and of the Lions, the bath which separates them, several of the gates and the mausoleum near the palace, belong to the time of Muhammad V (1354–9, 1362–91). Only one major construction, the interior of the Tower of the Infantas, is as late as the mid-fifteenth century.

The Alhambra itself is interesting in planning terms, displaying the combination of buildings and water, a conception carried far further in later Mughal gardens in India; but the Generalife, while containing some element of this, is much more a garden in Western terms, though still very much with water as its central theme. An inscription shows that the Generalife, a corruption of Jinnah al-Arif (for which two interpretations

OPPOSITE ABOVE *Plan showing the relative positions of the Alhambra and the Generalife overlooking Granada.*

OPPOSITE BELOW *Plan of the Generalife which, we are told, was restored by Sultan Ismail in 1319. Laid out on six levels, the garden was intended for use by the court during the summer and therefore contains numerous pavilions. The Sultana's Mirador is at the highest and coolest point.*

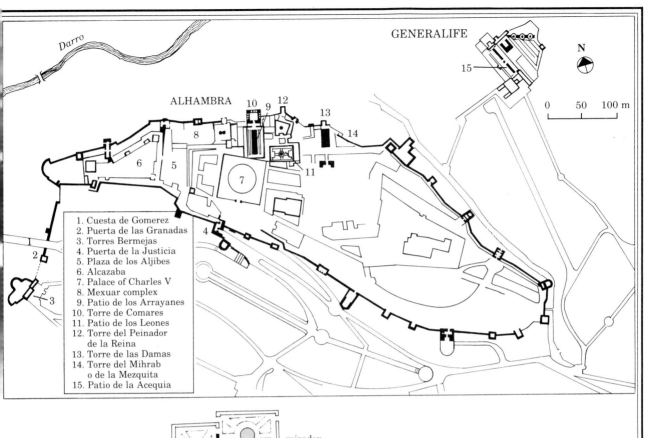

Darro

GENERALIFE

ALHAMBRA

N

0   50   100 m

1. Cuesta de Gomerez
2. Puerta de las Granadas
3. Torres Bermejas
4. Puerta de la Justicia
5. Plaza de los Aljibes
6. Alcazaba
7. Palace of Charles V
8. Mexuar complex
9. Patio de los Arrayanes
10. Torre de Comares
11. Patio de los Leones
12. Torre del Peinador
    de la Reina
13. Torre de las Damas
14. Torre del Mihrab
    o de la Mezquita
15. Patio de la Acequia

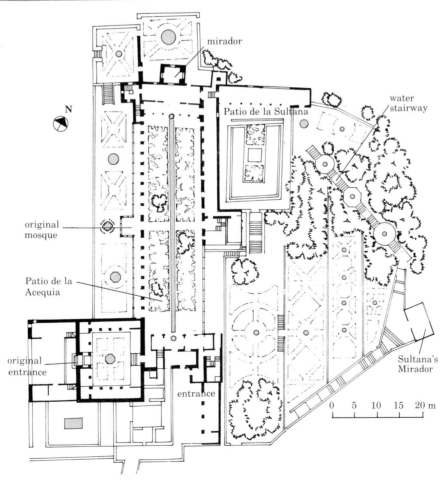

N

mirador

Patio de la Sultana

water
stairway

original
mosque

Patio de la
Acequia

original
entrance

entrance

Sultana's
Mirador

0   5   10   15   20 m

have been put forward, 'the Noblest of the Gardens' and 'Garden of the Architect'), was restored by Sultan Ismail in 1319, making it antedate most of the Alhambra buildings. However, there have been many later restorations of the building and modernizations of the garden.

The Generalife is approached from the Alhambra citadel across a bridge which spans the dividing ravine, then up a long cypress walk and through the creeper-clad thirteenth-century country house – still much as it was. This entrance through the house is typically Moorish. It leads into the Patio de la Acequia (Court of the Canal), perched on a terrace carved out of the hillside, with, on the left, a drop down to the ravine which is crossed by the path from the Alhambra and, on the right, more garden terraces mounting up to the Sultana's Mirador pavilion, the highest pinnacle of both complexes. The garden is first seen from within the gentle colonnade of the house, running away to another equally beautiful structure at the far end. On first glance it appears that a central canal is flanked by rather muddled modern planting on both sides. Fountains play from the sides of the canal towards the centre, reinforcing the perspective. On closer examination, however, one sees a cross-axis with at one end, in the centre of a connecting colonnade, what used to be a small mosque, and at the other a blank wall. The garden is therefore quadripartite in the typical Moorish tradition, the pool being an ablution tank for the little mosque.

James Dickie, the author of *The Hispano-Arab Garden*, states that the archaeologist Jesus Bermudez not only found the pavement of the original Arab paths underneath the accumulated debris of five centuries when excavating there in 1958, but also located the primitive level of the parterres (fifty centimetres below that of the paths) and even, pierced in the flanking paths of the watercourses, the outlet hole which made feasible the irrigation of the flower beds. Therefore the plan was of a quartered garden, or the Persian *chahar bagh*, such as Babur might have laid out in Agra or Shah Abbas at Isfahan. Green and white tiles were found bordering the path, and there was even evidence of confining basins, proving that all the trees in the garden were originally dwarfed.

A feature repeated again and again in the Alhambra and here in the Patio de la Acequia is the appearance of a water fountain set within a carved lotus bowl, sometimes fluted or sometimes inlaid. This motif, along with the fountain nozzles which represent tight lotus buds, must be of oriental origin, since the lotus does not grow in the south of Spain.

OPPOSITE *The Patio de la Acequia in the Generalife, looking back to the entrance pavilion. A quadripartite layout is retained by the path which crosses the centre of the canal and links the colonnades on the right to the terraces on the left.*

This, the oldest and most interesting garden part of the Generalife, is the main house complex, used for prayer, for entertaining and so on. Below it and looking back towards the Alhambra is another terrace in which are fountains encircled by box shrubs; this could be enjoyed from a colonnade under the one above linking the two pavilions and the projection of the little mosque, halfway along. Also at the lower level, and below the pavilion at the north end of the Patio de la Acequia, is yet another formal garden with a central pool. From this end there is a magnificent view to the Albaicin hill on the other side of the Darro river with its layered *carmen* gardens.

What used to be the harem is approached from the pavilion at the northern end and this overlooks its own little water court, known as the Patio de la Sultana. The canal shape here is in the form of a 'U' making a sort of water parterre round two central islands. Mrs Villiers-Stewart in *Spanish Gardens* states that this formerly ran through the building at the side and joined the canal in the main garden below. She goes on to say that the planting in this patio is simplicity itself, following the usual Eastern pattern of using one, or at most two, flowering plants to each little square or small enclosure. The garden should be seen in June, the month for which it was planned, when the court came up from the Alhambra. Then the oleanders that line the walls and crowd the islands are in bloom and the quiet harmony of the patio makes a perfect background for the flowing pink flowers under the cool greenery of surrounding cypresses.

Steps lead up from this garden into a rather forced, and undoubtedly later, box parterre, but from which leads the famous water stairway up to the top mirador, or lookout. On either side of the steps water runs in the tiled handrails, which turn into basins with fountain jets at the top and bottom of each flight. The flights are punctuated by landings with central fountains and shaded by pergolas of ancient Portuguese laurel. The Sultana's Mirador pavilion, approached up this cool watery staircase, commands a magnificent view back to the citadel with the Vega, or plain, beyond.

The Alhambra and Generalife occupy a natural acropolis, with on their north side a sheer fall of rock down to the Darro river, a tributary of the Guadalquivir. This gorge made an impenetrable defence. The towers that dot the north wall of the Alhambra above the cliff conceal habitations;

ABOVE LEFT *The Patio de la Sultana in the Generalife – small, intimate and alive with tinkling fountains to cool the summer's heat.*

ABOVE RIGHT *From a terrace above the Patio de la Sultana in the Generalife a unique stairway with handrails of gushing water and fountains at each level leads to the sultana's apartments at the top of the garden.*

they are not gateways. On the south side, looking towards the Vega, the Alhambra runs down to the present town. It was originally more or less bare – again for defensive purposes – but is now thickly wooded with elms planted for the benefit of the Duke of Wellington! The west end of this fortified rock is occupied by the Alcazaba (al-Qasbah), or citadel, with, rising to the east over a ravine, the sultan's summer residence of the Generalife. That the Generalife is only a quarter of an hour's walk away

53

from the Alhambra seems odd, but its position and siting is even more dramatic, being higher, cooler and therefore greener and ideal for summer. To the Western eye the courts of the Alhambra itself, percolated with pools and runnels of water, would seem cool enough, but, typical of all Muslim building, they are basically inward-looking (though they contain some stunning views outward also). One shudders to think what these buildings were like in winter for, lying below the Sierra Nevada, Granada does get cold, albeit for a short period. No doubt braziers and wall hangings with rich carpets underfoot and thicker clothing combated these elements.

In describing the Generalife before the Alhambra, one is perhaps putting the cart before the horse, but chronologically it appears that some at least of this structure was built first. The complex of the Alhambra is much

Plan of the Moorish palace of the Alhambra, with the public reception area on the left and the sultan's apartments and harem on the right.

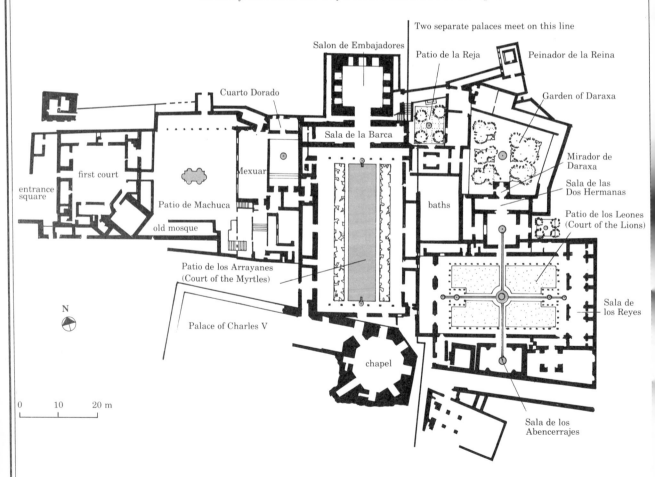

more compact than the Generalife, being broadly a building with open spaces in it, whereas the Generalife is a series of garden 'rooms' punctuated with pavilions. Pools and building are interlocked like beads along a watery thread, with visual changes of level down into other courtyards, the ins and outs of connecting passages, the elements of surprise, the delicate architecture, the sound of trickling water, and the vague wafting scent of orange blossom to complement it. It is truly the most sensuous place to which I have ever been, and in it one feels the excitement of the Orient, of proud Arabs swirling through courtyards and the dark-eyed beauties of the harem peering down from behind lattice screens. It has all been said many times before, none surpassing Washington Irving's *Tales of the Alhambra*, written at the height of the nineteenth-century romantic vogue for Islam. It is all still true, only more so, despite the presence of the ubiquitous tourist.

The enclosure of the Alhambra is divided into three parts, the hilltop's western plateau being the citadel which was the military headquarters for the whole complex. The second division, the central area, is occupied by the Alhambra palaces now joined, but housing at one time the sultan, his harem and a constant procession of the state's most important visitors. The last, eastern section was the royal city with its own shops, workshops, houses, baths, a *madrasa* (theological school) and a great mosque. Little of this area now remains.

Today the Alhambra is approached from the town below, up the Cuesta de Gomerez (Gomerez Hill), and through the sixteenth-century Puerta de las Granadas, or Gate of the Granadas, replacing an earlier Moorish one. The final grand entrance is through the Puerta de la Justicia, or Gate of Justice, further up the hill, so called because the sultans of Granada sat in judgement there. The gate, dated 1348, bears an inscription ending with the words, 'May the Almighty make this gate a protecting bulwark and may He write down its construction among the imperishable actions of the just.' Over the arch is an open hand which symbolizes the five basic tenets of Islam: belief in the oneness of God, prayer, fasting in the month of Ramadan, almsgiving and the *Hajj*, or pilgrimage to Mecca. Through this gate one continues upwards and crosses the Plaza de los Aljibes, or Place of the Cisterns – formerly tanks of water were stored here in case of siege – with the Alcazaba on the left and on the right the palace of Charles, which sits like a Renaissance cuckoo in a cosy Muslim nest, to come to the western end of the old palace. This area is known as the Mexuar complex, and is in reality a series of ruins or restored features with several courts. The larger court has a nondescript pool in the middle and is known as the Patio de Machuca, or Court of Machuca, this being the name of Charles V's architect who carried out many repairs.

Now through a long covered room, originally open to the west, known as the Mexuar, one enters the first of the original royal palaces. Whether this was originally the entrance or not seems in doubt. This leads to the first small court, the Patio del Mexuar, with a backing room known as the Cuarto Dorado (Golden Room). Suddenly one has moved from Spain to another world of Arabian Nights. In the centre of this little marble-floored court is a simple lotus pool and fountain, and behind it a magnificent wall covered in stucco decoration and pierced by two doors and five windows, surmounted by a *muqarnas* frieze (a *muqarnas* is a stalactite-like decoration). Much of the other decoration of the buildings throughout the Alhambra comprises written verse – quotations from the Quran and from contemporary poets. Ceilings, beams and doors are of carved wood, with floors and walls in marble or a mosaic of purple, green and orange glazed-earthenware tiles. The remaining surfaces are painted stucco, the colours usually being primary red, blue or yellow (which are important Sufi colours).

Through one of the doors in this tiny court one weaves a way through passages to come suddenly upon the famous Patio de los Arrayanes, or Court of the Myrtles, previously called the court of the palace and the court of ablutions for all who were present at the state ceremonial held in the private mosque nearby. The change of name reminds one of the change of royal owners since the former, infidel ceremonial use was banned. The court is rectangular with a long and narrow pool. At its southern end there is a simple portico in six columns with a central modern door, beyond which is Charles' building again.

It is the north end of this central court which is justifiably the most famous. It consists, externally in elevation, of an open portico with, behind, a long wall with corner towers and finally the background mass of the Torre de Comares (Comares Tower) – a wonderful architectural build-up, mirrored and enhanced by the simple pool of water, brimming and clear. The whole composition, utilizing the transition from plain, architecturally clipped myrtle to rich Moorish carving, is masterly.

OPPOSITE *Though familiar, the Court of the Myrtles in the Alhambra*
presents a breathtaking composition in which the richness
of Moorish architecture is offset by the simplicity
of a large reflecting pool and plain myrtle hedges.

The bull's eye, as it were, of this elevation leads one into another breathtaking series of rooms, first the Sala de la Barca (Hall of the Boat) whose function is not clear but whose name derives from its boat-shaped ceiling, and finally into the so-called Salon de Embajadores, or Ambassadors' Hall, within the Tower of the Comares. On plan, it is simply an empty space with three walls, each pierced by three openings, and a fourth side which looks back to the pool. These openings, lacking any apparent barrier, look down to the valley below. What in fact makes the composition so riveting is the decoration of the room: tiles and decorated

stucco cover the walls in blinding Moorish patterns, all covered by a beautiful wooden inlay ceiling. One cannot describe the simple pool of the garden alone in bright sunlight, for it belongs to the buildings which surround it and to their cool shaded interiors, and they belong to it as well. Their interrelation is complex; this feeling must have been even more obvious when viewed from floor level, as of course this is how the Ambassadors would see the room, sitting cross-legged on rich carpets, to be received by the sultan.

The Court of the Myrtles originally constituted the end of the palaces of the Alhambra. Beyond it, in a totally different style, lay another. The two were interconnected by the Catholic sovereign after their conquest to house the much larger court. This means that the visitor can now progress from the Court of the Myrtles into the Patio de los Leones (Court of the Lions). Again, one has seen photographs of this a hundred times, but the reality surpasses any pictorial reproduction.

With the Patio de la Acequia of the Generalife, the Court of the Lions is the only Arab garden extant in Granada. It was begun in 1377. When the courtyard was excavated to reinforce the foundations of the surrounding building, it was found that the original Arab level was eighty centimetres below the present one. It is presumed that this was for more than one purpose: firstly, it lent added prominence to the geometrical character of the enclosure; secondly, the vegetation could never attain such a height as would allow it to interfere with the architecture; and lastly, it converted the garden into a floral carpet, so that a person walking on a path at the level of the blossom had the illusion of treading upon a carpet woven with flowers instead of threads.

The court itself is in fact quite small, and its surrounding portico, a colonnade with two projecting pavilions, articulates the sides in an unusually complicated way, creating a forest of pillars. The layout has a Persian quality in that it is composed of crossed watercourses which, before they converge on the fountain basin supported by twelve lions, cool the surrounding rooms. Here they rise as jets and trickle in narrow canals down steps into the courtyard to be returned to the fountain before being spewed forth by the lions again. These famous central lions (twelve in number suporting the central fountain basin) seem crude in comparison to the building they so enhance, and are supposedly of Byzantine origin. The significance of carved lions, seen all over Islam, is threefold, according

OPPOSITE *Perhaps even more familiar and breathtaking than the Court of the Myrtles is the Court of the Lions in the Alhambra, which was begun in 1377.*
The plan is simple although the decoration is sumptuous, and the central fountain with its wild animals provides another arresting feature. On a metaphysical level the movement of water in four channels (creating a quartered paradise garden) towards the centre and out again from the fountain suggests the Islamic concept of expansion and contraction.

to Oleg Grabar. They were first a practical means of adornment; they were also symbols of princely power and victory; and lastly, on a higher level, they were the re-creations of a luxurious setting associated with Solomon and described by an eleventh-century Jewish poet, Ibn Gabirol, for in medieval Jewish and Muslim legend Solomon, the king-prophet, had become the prince *par excellence*. The poet refers to a throne inlaid with gold which was erected in honour of the Queen of Sheba and which had twelve lions (I Kings 10:18–20). Oleg Grabar states that this story and others related to it found artistic or architectural expression throughout much of Islam.

From excavated pollen samples we know that the garden was originally planted with orange trees. It has been suggested that these pre-dated the surrounding building, and when Philip le Beau visited the Alhambra in 1502 six of these were still left. The four plots subdivided by the canals were then gravelled over at some time, but recently some authority in its wisdom has replanted them with ground cover, presumably as a deterrent to tourists walking there.

At the eastern end of the court is the Sala de los Reyes, or Hall of the Kings. It is an open room running the length of the court but divided into three square, domed units, separated by enclosed rectangular spaces, making a magical succession of light and dark, but always accompanied by the sound of water from the courtyard.

On the south side is the Sala de los Abencerrajes (Ibn Sarraj), or Hall of the Abencerrajes, whose name derives from that of a family whose members were brutally murdered there towards the end of Muslim rule in Spain. The cool dark depth of the fountain pool in this room seems to reflect this rather sinister aspect. The room facing it is the most impressive of the complex, called the Sala de las Dos Hermanas, or Hall of the Two Sisters, in romantic memory of two captive sisters said to have died of longing at the sight of the amorous happenings they could see in the Jardin de Daraxa (Lindaraja), or Garden of Daraxa, below, but in which they could not participate! The hall is square with a *muqarnas* cupola set in an octagon, and on three sides the room is framed by long rectangular halls, two of which are unlit side rooms; the more northerly one, however, leads to a small, square and superbly ornate pavilion known as the Mirador (or lookout), which overhangs the Garden of Daraxa below. Sated with the visual pleasure of the Court of the Lions on one side and the aural pleasures

OPPOSITE ABOVE *A channel leads straight from the dark pool in the
Sala de los Abencerrajes in the Alhambra to the fountain
in the centre of the Court of the Lions.*

OPPOSITE BELOW *The Sala de los Reyes at the eastern end of the Court
of the Lions, showing the succession of light and dark
in its ravishingly gilded and decorated interior.*

of splashing fountains in the Daraxa below on the other, all overlaid with the heavy sensuous scent of orange blossom, one can easily commiserate with the two sisters!

In the westerly side room of the Hall of the Two Sisters there is a doorway which leads to the apartments occupied by the newly wed Charles V, following his arrival at the Alhambra in 1526. From this a gallery runs north-east to the Peinador de la Reina (Queen's Dressing Room). On one side there is the spectacular view down over the Darro to the Albaicin hill, while on the other there is a charming little patio known as the Patio de la Reja, or Court of the Grille. This patio and the neighbouring Garden of Daraxa with its royal apartments were entirely reconstructed in the sixteenth century and, even though some of their features may have been influenced by earlier Moorish building, they are not themselves old. Originally they may have been the living quarters of the palace or possibly even the celebrated harem, the thought of which has so titillated writers ever since the sixteenth century.

The Patio de la Reja was begun in 1654, but its feeling is entirely Moorish. It is covered with pebble mosaic and centres on a raised fountain guarded by a cypress marking each corner. From this little patio one goes through a colonnade, which surrounds the Daraxa like a cloister, to the garden itself. It is dominated by a beautiful fountain brought from the Mexuar by Charles V and mounted on a Renaissance pedestal. Since it is raised, one can see the underside of the Moorish basin which is scored and faceted and reflected in the pool below. The planting of the garden is the traditional pattern of paths bordered by box, with the beds planted with orange trees and sentinel cypresses round the fountain, their cool green a perfect foil to the glories of the buildings which they punctuate. Off to one side of the garden are the baths, which are of the classical Islamic type, but covered in exquisite tilework.

Located in higher ground to the east of the palace complex and approached from the Garden of Daraxa is the Partal, or site of the old royal city. It now consists of a large garden, a pool and portico with a single tower ending in a mirador overlooking the valley, all of the time of Yusuf I (1333–54). Seen on its own, this complex would be charming, but after the beauties of the palace complex it is curiously open and disappointing.

OPPOSITE *The Garden of Daraxa in the Alhambra, looking up to the window of the Sala de las Dos Hermanas. An arcade runs round three sides of the garden, and in the centre a Moorish fountain brought from the Mexuar by Charles V is raised on a Renaissance pedestal.*

COURTYARD GARDENS

Perhaps in Spain more than anywhere else the domestic garden form is important, as opposed to the palace tradition which one inevitably seeks out. For here the Islamic tradition strongly overlays the Roman urban house type, and the two combine to form the patio or enclosed court. But even the patio tradition has its variations, each one developing over the centuries in its own vacuum. For while khalifs, princes and men of learning travelled the length and breadth of the Mediterranean and beyond with seeming ease and speed, the peasant, except if he went on a pilgrimage, was generally confined to his own particular valley. His horizons were considerably narrower and his peculiar vernacular developed in isolation. So the patio of Cordoba is different from that of Seville; and in Granada, the other main town of al-Andalus, the enclosed courtyard garden extends above, below or at the side of the house. The *carmen*, as the latter type of garden is called, is unique in its form and much more a garden in Western terms, though, as in the rest of Islam, the houses were always inward-

ABOVE *Though built in 1654, the Patio de la Reja in the Alhambra has typically Islamic elements such as the floor pattern, whose flowing and interweaving shapes signify continuity and also form the star of Islam.*

looking, enclosed and private in character and focus.

The Cordoban type of patio is by far the simplest. The form of the house is typically an atrium, after the Roman prototype on which it must be based, with a central open area and surrounding cloister off which the rooms of the house lead. The storey above – and this is a development, since Roman houses were generally single-storeyed – follows the same pattern, so that the supporting pillars become an arcade. These pillars are often of stone and are of Roman origin, taken from ruins (of which there were many, as southern Spain was a thriving outpost of the Roman empire). The rest of the structure is of white or colour-washed adobe. The colonnades of these cool inward-looking dwellings are furnished, not at random with garden chairs as on a verandah, but with permanent heavy pieces, chests, a settee and pictures hung on the wall. The focal point of the house is the pebble-floored patio surrounding a simple pool, invariably with a trickling fountain. Around the pool, individual pots of flowers are grouped. The layout is both simple and charming, allowing subdued light into all the rooms of the house, but remaining a cool oasis at its very centre.

ABOVE *A typical patio in Cordoba with its surrounding cloister,*
the design of which was based on the Roman atrium. The scale is small and
intimate for summer living, with pieces of furniture
under the cloisters and plates hung on the walls.

In Seville the format of the houses is the same, but as it was the richest and last leading city of al-Andalus, the patios are grander, with more elaborate, often Mudejar, architectural detailing. The scale too is large, with higher arcades, and one patio may lead into another, so that the building is punctuated with watery courtyards. The pebblework of homely Cordoba gives way to marble flooring, and the simple potted plant becomes a more exotic palm. In the grander houses of Seville, reminiscent of those of Renaissance Italy, there are alternative rooms for winter and summer living. In winter the family lives upstairs, to catch the warmth of the sun. In summer, living is at the lower level in shaded coolness. At the Casa de las Duenas, a palatial Mudejar home of the Duchess of Alba, built some time after 1483, the summer dining-room faces one of the shaded patios on one side, and is then open at either end, looking one way into a small orange-filled garden and the other onto a trickling pool. Exquisite heavy Spanish furnishings and family portraits virtually blend with garden and water in an extremely grand inside-out arrangement.

Another beautiful feature of Spanish gardens, and nowhere more apparent than in Seville, is the ironwork *rejas*, or grilles, through which tantalizing glimpses lead one on into the next patio.

While equally private behind high walls when one is adjacent to them, the *carmen* gardens of Granada can be seen from across the ravine from the deep window recesses and balconies of the Alhambra as they step up the Albaicin hill, jammed in amongst the surrounding houses. They are easily identified by groups of tall cypresses which usually surround a central pool and which contrast with the horizontal lines of the houses. The garden is situated above, below or at the side of the house, and of course it always has a magnificent view back to the towers of the Alhambra and the Generalife with the snow-capped Sierra Nevada behind. Many date from Moorish times and are in the main formal, similar to medieval Western gardens, from which they probably evolved. Their pattern is dictated by the need for irrigation for the orange trees with which they are filled. Box-edged paths divide the area into four, eight or twelve sections with, at the junction of the paths, a small pool, sometimes surrounded by seating, or, where the pool is absent, bent-over cypresses or high hedges forming a little green room known as a *glorieta*. These *glorietas* are a standard feature in Spanish gardens and are the Moorish equivalent of the Persian and Mughal pavilion. Their use as romantic trysting-places

OPPOSITE *The central courtyard of the Palacio de las Duenas*
in Seville built in the fifteenth century in Mudejar style
and now belonging to the Duchess of Alba.

is legendary, but a more mundane function is as an outside dining-room. These *glorietas* are also the origin of the Western rose arbour, but are visually more successful since they seem sculpted out of the surrounding greenery, and not imposed on it as an architectural feature. The little pools and fountains at the intersection of the paths often take the form of the Moorish lotus basin, like those in the Alhambra.

While remaining a true garden rather than a patio, the *carmen* of Granada nevertheless retains the feeling of an outside room, with little views and openings clipped through the hedges. However, the clipping is softened and contrasted with tall cypress spires and the soft green of surrounding citrus. They are a study in green for much of the year, after spring's flush of iris, rose and wistaria, with the ever-present heady scent of orange blossom and jasmine and the trickle of water.

The Spanish garden has a much more ordered feel to it than those in Persia with which it may be compared, and is considerably tighter in conception than those of Mughal India. The basic layout of the Persian *chahar bagh* is, however, unmistakable.

ABOVE *A typical feature of the* carmen *gardens is the* glorieta, *a green pavilion of clipped cypresses resembling the later arbours of early European gardens.*

OPPOSITE *A profusion of cypress trees and overflowing greenery on the Albaicin hill opposite the Alhambra marks the presence of a* carmen *garden, jammed in among the Moorish-style houses and narrow winding alleys of this old Arab quarter.*

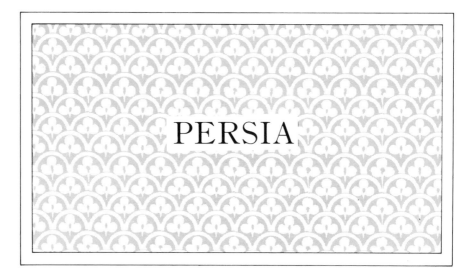

PERSIA

TIMURID EMPIRE

Only meagre descriptions of the Persian garden during the eleventh and twelfth centuries survive: one of the gardens of the eleventh-century Saljuq leader, Malik Shah I, the Bagh-i Bakr of Isfahan in Iran, was said to be fragrant with narcissus, myrtle and saffron, while its pavilion was provided with luxurious seating from which to enjoy the magnificent prospects to the accompaniment of cooing doves and cooling breezes. The Bagh-i Falasan possessed a lofty pavilion variegated in colour, with a high tower commanding a fine view over the garden which had vines growing in it and brimming streams. In the garden of Ahmed Siyah were beds of bay and myrtle, meadows with pools and places for sitting as well as lofty pavilions. The Bagh-i Karan was planted with fruit trees and rows of pines and cypresses and is described as having two pavilions, one overlooking the river and the other in front of the *maydan* (public open space) of the city. This garden was still known to exist in 1323. The pavilion with a commanding prospect is a common feature of them all, while the combination of fruit trees and shade-giving trees is a precursor of gardens to follow.

An early garden of which there is a more precise description is that of the Mongol Mahmud Ghazan Khan (1294–1304), laid out at Ujan near Tabriz in north-west Iran. Mongol intrusion into the Islamic world had

started as early as 1220 under the dreaded Jenghiz Khan. This garden was to provide a setting for the celebration of the completion of the copying of the Quran in 1302. Preparations had begun three years previously when a large square had been enclosed by a wall in order to provide 'a pleasant and agreeable meadow for the sojourn of the emperor'. Tanks and cisterns were installed to feed rivers and streams. Avenues were planted round the edge with willows to provide a passage for the populace, who had to be confined to the periphery of the enclosure, the central area being reserved

ABOVE *Jenghiz Khan giving an address in the mosque at Bukhara, from a Persian miniature of 1397.*

71

for the golden pavilion and the surrounding towers, baths and lofty buildings. The Mongols apparently developed this type of garden for a purpose peculiar to their own traditions, for the assumption of royal power required a garden setting for the nomadic encampment. This type of garden and the functions and customs within it passed to the warrior Timur Lenk.

We also know that Ghazan Khan was the architect of a complex two miles south of Tabriz at Sham, which in variety, magnitude and organization rivalled anything since Persepolis. Now only rubble, the buildings comprised *madrasas*, a hospital, library and administrative palace, observatory and summer palace as well as arcades and gardens of exceptional charm on which 14,000 workmen laboured for four years.

By 1394, Timur Lenk (meaning Timur the Lame), or Tamerlane, was in the heart of Persia, having swept with his warrior horsemen down from central Asia. He claimed direct descent from Jenghiz Khan and was the founder of the Timurid dynasty. In thirty-five years he campaigned as far north as Moscow, then south as far as Delhi and to the west against Ottoman Turkey. Timur left an endless trail of death and destruction, sparing only craftsmen from the fate of joining the countless pyramids of skulls which it was his gruesome custom to erect outside captured cities. These craftsmen he sent back to Samarkand, which he had created as his capital to become the focal point of eastern Islam. Samarkand is now within the boundary of the Soviet Union. Around and near Samarkand, Timur created a series of royal gardens of which we know a considerable amount, both through contemporary writers and, more particularly, Clavijo, a Spaniard who went to Samarkand in 1404 as Ambassador of the King of Castile and Leon. A century later Babur (1483–1530), himself a conqueror and emperor and the founder of the Mughal dynasty, wrote of these gardens of Timur, which then still existed. We know from miniatures painted at this time that these descriptions were true, and the form of the gardens can also be seen in early carpet design. As Clavijo approached Samarkand, he noted: '... so numerous are the gardens and vineyards surrounding Samarkand that a traveller who approaches the city sees only mountainous height of trees, and the houses embowered amongst them remain invisible.' Donald Wilber, an early writer on the Persian garden, has reconstructed in his *Persian Gardens and Garden Pavilions* a plan of the gardens which surrounded the city at that time, combining the

OPPOSITE *Timur presiding over a meeting of tribal chiefs in a garden outside Samarkand in 1404, from a Persian miniature of 1523.*

descriptions of Babur and other contemporary commentators with a nine-teenth-century map of the city, which showed all the watercourses and canals constructed by Timur and his grandson Ulugh Beg, which must have fed many gardens.

Babur describes in his *Baburnama* one garden that was built on a small hill and included a variety of different plots laid out on a regular plan in terraces, in which elms, cypresses and white poplar were planted in the numerous compartments. This is perhaps the first mention of the *chahar bagh*, or quartered garden, in Persia, although its existence was known of previously in earlier Muslim gardens of al-Andalus.

The formal relationship between the town of Samarkand and the royal garden in which the Black Throne was situated, as Babur describes it, precedes that of Safavid Isfahan, for from the Firuz or Victory Gates a stately avenue was planted on each side with pine trees, which led directly to the Bagh-i Dilgusha, or Garden of Heart's Ease. (Incidentally, the royal garden was so large that one of the builders of the palace lost his horse within it and it grazed there for six months before it was found.) It was within this garden that Clavijo described his first audience with Timur, who was then seventy and nearly blind. Clavijo says:

We were come to a great orchard, with a palace therein . . . some distance without the city. Attendants took charge of us, holding each ambassador under his armpit, and led us forward, entering the orchard by a wide and very high gateway, most beautifully ornamented with tile-work in gold and blue. . . . We came to where a certain great lord of the court, a very old man, was seated on a raised dais . . . and we all made our obeisance. Then passing on we came before another dais where we found seated several young princes, the grandsons of his Highness, to whom we likewise paid our respects.

Then coming to the presence beyond we found Timur and he was seated under what might be called a portal . . . but upon a raised dais before which there was a fountain that threw up a column of water into the air backwards, and in the basin of the fountain there were floating red apples. His Highness had taken his place on what appeared to be a small mattress stuffed thick and covered with embroidered silk cloth, and he was leaning on his elbow against some round cushions that were heaped up behind him. He was dressed in a cloak of plain silk without any embroidery, and he wore on his head a tall white hat on the crown of which was displayed a ruby.

Donald Wilber describes this garden in more detail:

In 1396 Timur ordered that a garden should be constructed in the meadow known as the House of Flowers, the garden which he was later to name *Dilgusha*, or Heart's Ease. Astrologers selected a propitious day for the work to begin, and artists prepared plans which would regulate the alley and provide for the layout of flowerbeds. The area was plotted with perfect symmetry and provided with alleys, square beds and little wildernesses of various shapes. Sycamore trees were planted along the edges of the alleys and the remaining areas with fruit trees and flowering trees and bushes. After the garden proper was established, architects took over [there's something that could be learnt today] and provided high portals in the middle of each walled side, each one stretching some 2,500 feet. Within each corner area a small tile-covered pavilion was erected, and at the centre of the ensemble a palace three storeys in height was built.

In the same year Timur brought architects from Fars, Azerbaijan, Baghdad and Damascus to compete for the planning of a new palace to be built within his Bagh-i Shimal, or Northern Garden, lying to the north of Samarkand. Near the end of his life he ordered the building of another palace in a garden to the south of the Bagh-i Shimal, and within the building were basins of water and fountains of various forms. The garden itself was the one in which Clavijo was lodged when awaiting his first audience and may have been called Gul Bagh, or Rose Garden. He has described the garden in detail:

We found the garden to be enclosed by a high wall which in its circuit may measure a full league around, and within it is full of trees of all kinds save only limes and citron-trees which we noted to be lacking. Further, there are six great tanks, for throughout the orchard is conducted a great system of water, passing from end to end; while leading from one tank to the next they have planted five avenues of trees, very lofty and shady, which appear as streets, for they are paved to be like platforms. These quarter the orchard in every direction, and off the five main avenues other smaller roads are led to variegate the plan. In the exact centre there is a hill, built up artificially with clay brought thither by hand; it is very high and its summit is a small level space that is enclosed by a palisade of wooden stakes. Within this enclosure are built several very beautiful palaces, each with its complement of chambers magnificently ornamented in gold and blue, the walls being panelled with tiles of these and other colours. This mound on which the palaces have been built is encircled below by deep ditches that are filled with water, for a runlet from the main stream brings this water which flows into these ditches with a continuous and copious supply. To pass up into this hillock to the level of the palaces they have made two bridges. . . .

Many details about the household of Timur and its organization have been preserved, but, as Donald Wilber points out, of individuals laying out the gardens little is known, although there are references to architects who planned palaces and pavilions. Since these came from greater Iran it is natural to infer that these Samarkand gardens reflected prevailing Persian tradition; however, features from China and India were also in evidence. Chinese porcelain covered the walls, and the use of papier-mâché and interlaced patterns in wood strips reflected Chinese models, while the tradition of wainscoting or walling in the finest marbles was of Indian origin.

Timur was succeeded by one of his sons, Shah Rukh, who moved his

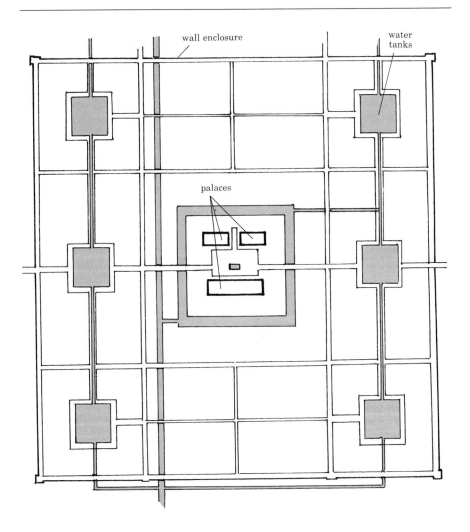

focal point of politics and culture down to Herat in what is now Afghanistan. During the reign of Sultan Husayn Baikara, who ruled from 1470 to 1506, a high point was reached in the arts at Herat. Babur spoke later of this golden age, writing of Herat and what happened in it, for he stayed in many of the gardens which Sultan Husayn had made and visited many others. Babur, we learn, proclaimed himself emperor in 1508 in a garden. Soon after his enthronement he ordered the building of a *chahar bagh* called the Bagh-i Jahan Ara near the shrine of Gazur Gah at Herat, but the garden no longer exists, although the shrine does. This garden, Babur tells us, covered forty hectares and its features included a palace, pools and masses of red tulips and roses. Babur was himself a horticulturalist and introduced fruits and plants to areas where they had been unknown.

The gardens at both Samarkand and Herat had similar forms: the division of the enclosed area into quarters; the use of the main water axis; the choice of a natural slope or the creation of an artificial hill in order to ensure the proper flow of water; and a mixture of the utilitarian vineyard and orchard with the pleasure garden. This combination became the prototype, described first by Clavijo and later by Babur, and was taken west to the Iranian plateau, and east to India with Babur himself.

THE SAFAVIDS AND AFTER

The Timurids, centred on Samarkand and then Herat (in the east of Iran), were superseded by the Safavids who came to power by seizing Tabriz in the north-west in 1499. The Safavids were the first truly native dynasty for more than a thousand years to rule Persia.

The Safavids were to play an important role as patrons of the arts throughout the sixteenth and seventeenth centuries, Shah Ismail and his successor Shah Tahmasp being well-known for their patronage of miniature painting. But it was not until Shah Abbas I the Great (1587–1629), transferred his capital to Isfahan in 1598 that an era of unsurpassed splendour and prosperity was inaugurated, to last the best part of a century. Shah Abbas was undoubtedly influenced by Timurid architecture, painting and calligraphy.

OPPOSITE *Reconstructed plan of the walled Gul Bagh, or Rose Garden,*
in Samarkand, where the Spanish envoy, Clavijo, was received by Timur in 1404.
The central pavilions stood on a hill and were surrounded
by canals of water. The rest of the garden, which boasted
three great decorative tanks of water on each side, was quartered
by avenues of trees, and presumably contained roses as well.

ISFAHAN

The focal point of Shah Abbas' city was the central square, known as the Maydan-i Shah, or Imperial Square, used for markets, spectaculars in the Roman style (including wild beast fights), court pageants and the playing of polo which was native to this part of the world. Round this square, Abbas sited his major buildings: to the south, the great royal mosque, Masjid-i Shah, a magnificent conception based on Timurid models with a jewel-like finish encrusted with mosaic; to the north, the royal bazaar linked through to the old city; on the east a smaller though no less magnificent mosque for the ladies of the court, the Masjid-i Shaykh Lutfullah, facing a strange small building known as the Ali Qapu, or Lofty Gateway, a seven-storey building which acted as a state gateway to Shah Abbas' paradise gardens beyond, but on top of which was an audience chamber and grandstand overlooking the *maydan*. The Ali Qapu thus became a link between the palace complex and the rude public world of the *maydan*.

Donald Wilber quotes a description of a reception given by Shah Abbas for foreign ambassadors at the Ali Qapu, for, being foreigners, they would be allowed no further:

' ... twelve of the Shah's finest horses, six on each side, harnessed with bridles inlaid with emeralds, rubies and gold enamel. The saddles were strewn with precious stones and each wore a cloth of gold brocade covered with pearls. The horses were tethered by ropes of coloured silk and gold to two stakes. Thirty paces from the horses were savage beasts reared to fight with young bulls: two lions, a tiger, and a leopard each lying on a fine large rug. Before them were two great basins of gold from which they fed. Near at hand were two gazelles and to the left two elephants crowned with canopies of gold brocades. There was also a rhinoceros!' The ambassadors ascended to the porch, their attendants bearing presents for the Shah. The Russian ambassador offered a huge glass chandelier, mirrors with painted frames, fifty fine furs and twenty bottles of vodka. The ambassador from the King of Bosra presented an ostrich, a young lion and three fine Arabian horses. As the presents were handed over, drums and trumpets sounded and the combats of wild beasts began in the *maydan*. [Up on the balcony there was feasting with] 'first a refreshment consisting of fresh and dried fruits, jams and liquids ... brought around. It was served in great lacquered trays, each of which held a nest of twenty or thirty little porcelain dishes. At the end of the porch was a huge buffet, one side holding fifty great bottles of wine and on the

---

OPPOSITE *A plan of Isfahan at the height of its splendour during the early seventeenth century.*

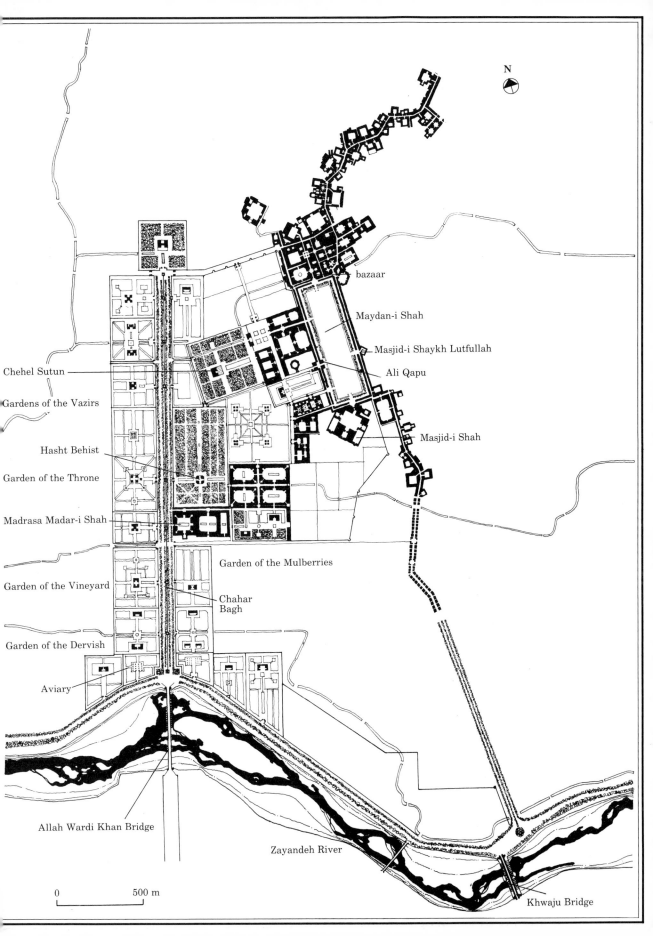

N

bazaar

Maydan-i Shah

Masjid-i Shaykh Lutfullah

Chehel Sutun

Ali Qapu

Gardens of the Vazirs

Hasht Behist

Masjid-i Shah

Garden of the Throne

Madrasa Madar-i Shah

Garden of the Mulberries

Garden of the Vineyard

Chahar
Bagh

Garden of the Dervish

Aviary

Allah Wardi Khan Bridge

Zayandeh River

Khwaju Bridge

0   500 m

other scores of cups. The Shah and his nobles drank draughts of wine and the Russian ambassador vodka!' Unfortunately, on this occasion the Russian was not able to hold his liquor. Forced by urgent necessity, he snatched off his tall fur headgear and held it in his hand as a basin. [Worse was to come for when] helped to take his leave he thrust his hat back on his head to the mingled delight and disgust of the company!

The *piano nobile* of Ali Qapu was a throne room, facing outwards to the *talar* and supported on massive wooden columns, from which the shah could watch the proceedings in the *maydan* below. The central feature of this great balcony was a rectangular marble basin, lined with lead sheets, in which three fountains played, fed by water raised by means of hydraulic machines driven by oxen. The pool today stands empty.

Little remains of the paradise gardens to which Ali Qapu originally led; the building or pavilion known as Chehel Sutun does still exist, though no longer approached through the Lofty Gateway. This grandiose building was a ceremonial pavilion within the garden, built by Shah Abbas II and designed to be used for state occasions, particularly for the reception of foreign embassies. Their approach to it however would not have been through Ali Qapu or the gardens. *Chehel Sutun* means 'forty columns', or alternatively 'many columns', but the *talar* of the palace has no more than twenty – the reflection of those in the vast rectangular pool on to which it faces doubling their number to forty. One can well imagine the magnificence of the shah's receptions there, held in a blaze of splendour.

The surrounding gardens of the Chehel Sutun are formal and grand, with lofty chenars and poplars shading cool areas of lawn beneath. They are all that remain of the royal garden, into which few were privileged to go, although, for those so favoured, they offered a delightful expanse of woods and gardens, pools and fountains and blue-tiled channels of running water. In one section of the enclosure four charming pavilions were sited amongst the trees; they were known as the Guest House, the Building of Paradise, the Hall of Mirrors and the Building of the Sea. These structures were reported to have been 'made expressly for the purpose of love, and the furnishings of each part are the most magnificent in the world, and the most voluptuous, with retreats that are nothing but an entire bed. All conveniently sited close by the harem complex.'

Shah Abbas' grand processional way to his city was known as the Chahar Bagh, or Four Gardens (the name is derived from the four vineyards which originally occupied the site). Strangely, this 'Champs Elysées' of Isfahan

OPPOSITE ABOVE *An 1867 engraving of the* maydan, *or central square, of Isfahan with the Royal Mosque in the middle and on the right the Ali Qapu, or Lofty Gateway, which led into Shah Abbas' paradise garden.*

OPPOSITE BELOW *The throne room on the upper floor of the Ali Qapu, from where Shah Abbas could have watched polo being played in the* maydan *in front of him or, to his right, seen the shimmering blue cupola of his mosque, as shown here.*

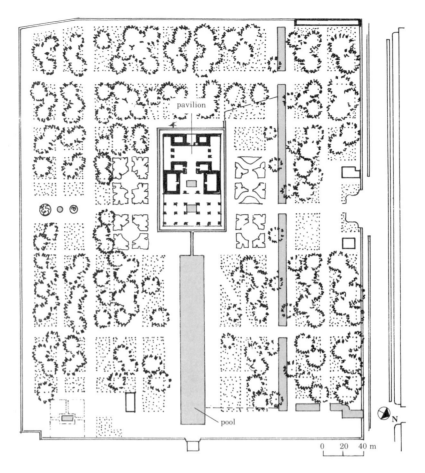

pavilion

pool

0 20 40 m

N

ABOVE *Plan of the Chehel Sutun in Isfahan, completed in 1647, with its central pavilion, reflecting pool and surrounding garden.*

OPPOSITE ABOVE *The interior of the Chehel Sutun in an 1840 engraving, looking out through the great columned* talar *to the gardens and the Royal Mosque in the distance.*

does not lead to the *maydan* but came to an end at a point west of the palace area, where it was as much a promenade as an avenue. However at the other end, where it crosses the Zayandeh river over the magnificent thirty-three-arch bridge known as the Allah Wardi Khan, it becomes a thoroughfare and a link to other royal gardens and to the Armenian Christian township which Shah Abbas created at Julfa.

OPPOSITE BELOW *An 1867 engraving of the Ayina Khaneh, or Hall of Mirrors, in Isfahan, which originally lay south of the Zayandeh River but was destroyed at the end of the nineteenth century. As in the Chehel Sutun the columned* talar *projects out from a series of rooms and was used for receptions.*

Leading from the Chahar Bagh was a complex of other gardens, erected by courtiers to Shah Abbas but now all vanished. At one time these gardens languished under provocative names like Garden of the Nightingale (they still sing in Isfahan), Garden of the Throne, Garden of the Vineyard, the Mulberries, Dervishes and so on. From these gardens, grandees and their entourages would throng the Chahar Bagh, trying to outdo each other in their pomp and munificence. It was ideally suited for this fashionable parade, for down the centre of the avenue, fifty metres wide, flowed a canal lined with cut stone, the water in it dropping at intervals, and punctuated with pools and fountains. In summer months these tanks of water were filled with cut heads of roses floating on the surface. On either side of the canal were a row of chenars, a promenade, then parterres filled with shrubs and flowers, then another row of chenars, the planting of which Shah Abbas personally supervised, placing a gold coin at the root of each sapling.

Chardin wrote that it was the most beautiful avenue he had ever seen; and it retained this charm until near the end of the nineteenth century, when many of the fine old plane trees were cut down. Lord Curzon, Viceroy of India, who also travelled widely in Persia, knowing of the Chahar Bagh in its prime, wrote:

But now [1892], what a tragical contrast. The channels are empty, their stone borders crumbled and shattered, the terraces are broken down, the parterres are unsightly bare patches, the trees, all lopped and pollarded, have been chipped or hollowed out or cut down for fuel by the soldiery of the Zil, the side pavilions are abandoned and crumbling to pieces, and the gardens are wildernesses. Two centuries of decay could never make the Champs Elysées in Paris, the Unter den Linden in Berlin or Rotten Row in London look half as miserable as does the ruined avenue of Shah Abbas.

Another ruin, though one now in the process of restoration, is the Hasht Behist (Eight Paradises), a small pleasure pavilion which stands in what was the Bagh-i Bulbul, or Garden of the Nightingale. It was built by a successor of Shah Abbas, Shah Sulaiman I, in 1670 and was much re-fashioned under the Qajar Fath Ali Shah. However, the building still evokes what many of the pleasure pavilions on the Chahar Bagh must have looked like. The octagonal plan of the Hasht Behist was not an unusual one, but an addition was the curious treatment of its corners. Each contains a pile of rooms, one on top of another, which become

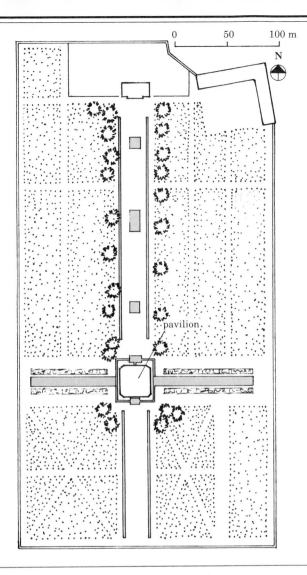

pavilion

enormous piers for the roof over a lofty central hall. Rooms were pierced with openings and galleries looking inside to the centre well, and with windows looking outwards to the garden as well. Each of the rooms was said to have had its own decoration, some with basins with fountains fed by lead pipes embedded in the walls; others had ceilings and walls entirely lined with mirrors. In the central well of the building were a pool and fountain; running out from this, down stepped water chutes called *chadars* (which occur again in Mughal gardens), were canals which extended out

ABOVE *Plan of the Hasht Behist, or Eight Paradises (built in 1670), in Isfahan, the only garden and pavilion left of the many gardens which once ran along the Chahar Bagh avenue. Water flowed out from the central octagonal pavilion on four sides.*

85

into the garden itself. The whole effect must have been highly decorative and a typical inside-out room for summer pleasure.

While remaining an extremely decorative garden pavilion, the Hasht Behist is also important, for it embodies many of the ideas central to Islamic cosmology. We have discussed the concept of centrifugal thrust as a common motif of the *chahar bagh*, here emphasized by the canals extending out from the building, but concurrent with this is the significance of the octagonal shape of the pavilion and its position in the centre of the garden. The importance of eight is stressed over and over again, in the eight-pointed-star pattern, for instance, and in the recurrence of the octagon which represents the eight paradises, surpassing the number of the seven spheres, and larger than hell which has seven storeys, proving that God's mercy is greater than His wrath. Also eight angels support the throne of God. This importance of the number eight is seen not only in pavilions and pattern, but often in tombs as well: the central chamber of the Taj Mahal, for instance, is eight-sided.

Practically adjacent to the old Garden of the Nightingale, and leading directly from the Chahar Bagh, is a late Safavid building called the Madrasa Madar-i Shah, or the Theological College of the Mother of the Shah. It was built between 1706 and 1714 as a series of rooms two storeys high, round a long marble-edged tank of water. On entering the courtyard from the noisy street outside, through wooden doors covered in silver and partly gilded, one passes through a lofty vaulted octagonal chamber, with a huge stone basin for ritual ablution in the centre. Beyond this at a lower level runs the pool with, on either side, the cool calm of the courtyard under lofty chenars making a striking contrast to the bustle outside. The surrounding arcaded buildings, beautifully restored, lead into the arcaded rooms in which the students were lodged. On the south side of the courtyard is the mosque, a tall *ivan* (arched entrance chamber) topped by two minarets fronting a dome chamber; the dome is covered with arabesques in black, yellow and white on a turquoise background, while on the *ivan* beneath the dome bands of blue are contrasted. While the whole conception is brilliantly coloured, it is crisp and cool, and surprisingly reminiscent of an Oxford quad.

Next to the Madrasa Madar-i Shah is a modern hotel, the Shah Abbas, situated within a converted caravanserai and sited originally to provide income for the *madrasa*. The courtyard here has been translated into a

OPPOSITE *An 1867 engraving of the interior of the Hasht Behist, showing the galleries and openings of the upper rooms, and the central fountain which repeats the octagonal shape of the building.*

*A view from the entrance up the central canal of the
Madrasa Madar-i-shah, or Theological College of the Mother of the Shah,
in Isfahan, which was completed in 1714.*

modern garden for the residents of the hotel, but still manages to retain much of the charm of its neighbour. Both these buildings were completed only six years before Isfahan was captured by the Afghans, and miraculously they survived the holocaust of that period.

With the demise of the Safavids in the mid-eighteenth century comes the end of the great period of Persian architecture, though not of garden building. While Isfahan represents the full flowering of Shah Abbas' inspiration, other shrine cities also benefited from his patronage, in particular Mahan, Mashhad and Qum.

ABOVE *The garden of the Shah Abbas hotel,*
formerly the courtyard of a caravanserai which
was attached to the Madrasa Madar-i-shah.

SHIRAZ

During the Afghan period, the leader of an important tribal grouping in the north-east of Persia made himself ruler. He was Nadir Shah and he went on to invade India, getting as far as Delhi. On his death, with the country in turmoil and exhausted from war, Muhammad Karim Khan Zand again united most of it under his rule, making his new capital at Shiraz. However, he ruled only as *vakil*, or regent. Karim Khan Zand's major architectural contribution to Persia was the building of the Vakil Mosque at Shiraz together with a fine bazaar, some caravanserais and other buildings; however, he also established the city as a direct trading link with the Persian Gulf, bringing to it prosperity and a wave of domestic building with their attendant gardens. Prior to this Chardin, who had visited Shiraz in 1674, noted that it was full of gardens 'which contain the largest trees of their kind in the world . . . cypresses, plane trees and pines'. It is also worth noting that two of the most famous Persian poets, Sadi (1213–92) and Hafiz (1320–92), both lived in Shiraz; their writings contain continual references to gardens. Karim Khan Zand built gardens for the tombs of both poets. Little remains of the Zand palace, however, though there is still a pretty octagonal pavilion set in a quartered garden with a large canal of water running from it.

The Zands were also the builders of the Bagh-i Dilgusha, which has its own *qanat*. The resultant avenues and orchards of orange trees, with pools and fountains, were famous. The garden still exists, as do two other gardens, the Haft Tan and Chehil Tan; but many other Zand gardens have now vanished.

One of the characteristics of house and mosque decoration of this period was the use of much stronger-coloured painted tilework, utilizing strong pinks with acid yellows; another was the vigorous quality of some of the designs which exactly reproduced carpet patterns of the period and prefaced the decadence of the succeeding Qajar period of 1779–1924. Late Qajar princes also took Shiraz to their hearts and built gardens round their palaces, for the city had by then recovered from its decline.

By the end of the nineteenth century, although Shiraz was by no means opulent again, it was regarded with affection by both Persians and travellers, part of this being due, no doubt, to the first impressions they would have had of the city. Shiraz is situated at the end of a long and

narrow valley. The valley wall above the city is broken by a gorge, and entrance to it was through a gate, in the second storey of which was a Quran of miraculous powers and which, it is said, passed down a benediction. At the same time the first view of the city opened out below: a spread of green on the valley floor, hatched across in brown by the tops of clay walls and, near the centre and rising up above the rest, the pale green bloom of a shrine dome. Around the edges of the green there were long files of cypresses and, up the near slopes of the hills, terraces of vineyards. Above lay the burning blue of the Persian sky. To travellers, after perhaps many days in the desert, it truly looked a paradise.

Down in the city itself, travellers found a modest and pleasing landscape: narrow walled lanes passed among vineyards and orchards, and by long, flat-roofed, clay houses. There was a handsome bazaar, and the remains

ABOVE *A small octagonal pavilion and adjoining canal in a garden full
of Banksian roses and cypress trees is all that remains of a former
royal garden in Shiraz belonging to Karim Khan Zand (reigned 1750–79).*

of the pleasant Zand palace complex, the shrine with a gold finial at the top, a square and a fort with a tower at each corner and storks' nests. The most pleasing feature of Shiraz, however, was its large gardens, over thirty of them, a surprising number for so small a city, and each with its own pavilion. In addition there were the tomb gardens of famous dervishes and the poets, which in the local custom were places of resort. The city too was favoured by a good climate with sunny temperate winters and summers, cooled by trees and open water channels. Even the products of Shiraz read like the foods of paradise: limes and honey, wine and grain.

Some of the Qajar gardens of Shiraz were terraced in a manner similar to those of Mughal India. Donald Wilber describes the Bagh-i Takht, which developed from an existing site, described in 1665, and was probably revamped to its present, though decadent, state by the Qajar ruler, Muhammad Shah, in about 1789. It is a garden of descending levels, rather in the style of Italian Renaissance gardens, and has a natural watercourse descending across them, ending in a great formal pool. Wilber said that

BELOW LEFT *Plan of the Bagh-i Takht, Shiraz, which was mainly developed in 1789 by the Qajar ruler Muhammad Shah.*

BELOW RIGHT *Plan of the Bagh-i Eram, Shiraz, a large Qajar garden with a strong linear form, which was laid out in 1824.*

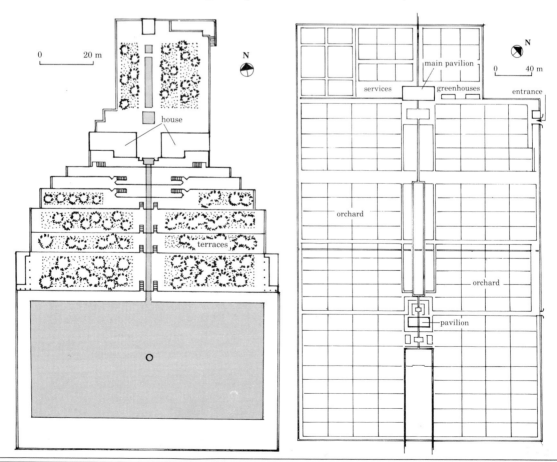

such a pool was called *dariacheh*, or 'little sea', and it is certain that it was made as large as possible. Descriptions emphasize that all such pools were provided with small boats; in them the proud owners navigated across the 'sea', leaving their arid shores far behind. This type of hillside garden also appears in Azerbaijan and again in India where Persian influence may have been grafted on to the plans established by Babur. There is no way of knowing, however, when this type of garden appeared in Persia.

Another preserved Qajar garden is the Bagh-i Eram, which was laid out in 1824 and contains another descending watercourse on a quite massive scale, bordered by an avenue of stately cypresses, with groves of orange trees on either side. An unfortunate modern rose garden has been laid out to one side of the house, but this in no way destroys the original garden layout. The house, taking the place of the pavilion, is the focal point of the layout, and is a typical nineteenth-century dwelling in which Western influences have been adapted in a typical Persian way. There are in fact a considerable number of these Qajar houses left in Shiraz; most, of at

The central pavilion of the Bagh-i Eram, which has been converted during this century to hold modern windows. The central canal still flows, although a modern rose garden has been introduced on one side of the pavilion.

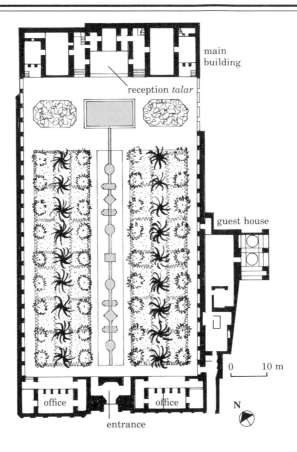

main building

reception *talar*

guest house

0   10 m

office

office

entrance

N

least middle-class status, have their own pool, and this is a continuing tradition. Intense summer heat is allayed in them by running open water channels through the house, and by pools and fountains, as well as the use of wind towers (*badgir*), which aerate basement chambers. Such a house, containing some of these features, is the Narangistan in Shiraz.

Begun in the 1870s, the Narangistan one now sees (housing the Asia Institute) is the traditional Persian *biruni*, connected to a neighbouring building which was formerly the women's quarters. The house was built for the Qavam family, who came to the city in the mid-eighteenth century, and who eventually rose to serve the Qajar court in Tehran. At the time of its building, the Qavams also maintained two country houses, so this was essentially a town house, designed for opulence and show. The Persian *biruni* serves three purposes. First of all, it is a place of business, an office. (Because Persian families are large and they may and do engage in a

ABOVE *Plan of the Narangistan in Shiraz, a typical* biruni, *or town house, which was built in the 1870s. It consisted of offices, a guest house, and living quarters with a reception* talar, *all set around a garden with trees and a series of pools linked by a central canal.*

94

The garden and entrance building of the Narangistan,
Shiraz, as seen from the main building.

variety of enterprises, these offices were extensive and always of much importance.) Secondly, a *biruni* is a place of ceremonious reception in a full and formal sense; lastly, it is a guest house, provided with sleeping quarters.

The original offices of the Narangistan are to be found immediately to the left and right after passing through the entry vestibule from the street. Thus in the old days, Persians calling on purely business matters were not required or encouraged to go to the reception and guest quarters which lay beyond. The offices consisted of half a dozen rooms fronted by verandahs, which served as waiting rooms, and the large garden, extending north from the verandah but fenced and gated off from the main building at the end, served the same purpose. Here people might stroll or sit under a tree awaiting their turn, for the accomplishment of business in Persia can take a long time. Guests arriving for a daytime reception, or intending to stay, went straight up the avenue of orange trees which bisects the garden and gives the place its name, towards the main building which is slightly raised on a terrace containing a large reflecting pool.

A little beyond this and above, occupying the whole centre of the main building, is the great reception *talar*, roofed and pillared, and open to the garden. Most of the walls and ceiling are covered with mosaic mirror work, so that whether it was daytime and sunlit or night-time when the three-tiered chandeliers were lit, the visitor arriving through the garden saw at the end of the long vista a great blaze of light. The *Qavam al-Mulk*, the master, the provider, the very incarnation of all this light, sat in a small room at the rear of the *talar* (as Shah Abbas must have sat at the rear of the Chehel Sutun); this room was entirely faced with mosaic mirror work, so giving the impression of being the interior of an enormous gaudy jewel. Light has always meant much to Persians, be it fire, the sun and moon, mirrors and gems or the reflecting surfaces of pools; it also plays an important part in the language, particularly in old forms of address: 'Sublime Sovereign whose standard is the sun, whose splendour is that of the firmament', 'Exalted like the planet Saturn', 'Footpath of heaven' etc. Leading off the *talar* are several extensions to the reception area, consisting of four second-storey rest rooms, each of which has a large window looking down into the *talar*, not unlike those of the Hasht Behisht. The guest and reception quarters are completed by a half-basement summer room.

In terms of their purpose as an office, a reception area and a guest house

OPPOSITE ABOVE *The view from the 'new gardens' of the Generalife, Spain, looking towards Granada, with the towers of the Alhambra on the left and the Albaicin hill on the right.*

OPPOSITE BELOW *The gardens of the Partal in the Alhambra, with the Partal itself, known as the Torre de las Damas, or Tower of the Ladies, in the background.*

ABOVE *This view of the Patio de la Acequia in the Generalife,
looking from above the entrance pavilion to the mirador at the end,
gives a clear idea of the garden's quadripartite division.*

OPPOSITE *The window in the Sala de las Dos Hermanas in the Alhambra
from which two captive sisters are said to have seen amorous happenings
in the Garden of Daraxa below.*

ABOVE *The Chehel Sutun, Isfahan, Iran. It is thought that
the doubling of the building's twenty columns by their reflection in the pool in front
of them explains the name* chehel sutun, *which means 'forty columns'.*

OPPOSITE *A patio in Cordoba, Spain, with a central pool and surrounding cloister*

ABOVE *The secondary pavilion at the Bagh-i Fin, Kashan, Iran, with its
pool from which water is fed along blue-tiled canals into the garden.*

OPPOSITE ABOVE *The inner courtyard of the Madrasa Madar-i Shah, Isfahan,
Iran, with its dome and minarets in the background and to each side the
two-storeyed arcades which open into rooms for teachers and students.*

OPPOSITE BELOW *The reception talar (shaded by great canvas curtains) and living quarters
of the Narangistan at the end of the main garden approach.*

the building and garden were well planned; ornament and function do not preclude each other, and the building with its garden remains both romantic and practical. Further, the Narangistan contains both balance and variety, for from every room, one looks out onto the water of the pool and canal, framed with orange trees, and across the palms and tulip domes of the city beyond to the mountains.

OTHER PERSIAN GARDENS

Other centres of Qajar building included Tabriz, Kashan (Bagh-i Fin) and Tehran, which began to gain in importance as a city in 1788, when Aga Muhammad Khan, the founder of the dynasty, made his capital there. At Tabriz we have a record of a garden known in the fourteenth century as the Hasht Behist, probably built by the ruler Uzan Hasan, and with a central structure not unlike that of its later namesake at Isfahan. There are two gardens in Tabriz today from the Qajar period. The smaller is that at Fathabad, where a long water canal punctuated by pools runs through an orchard, terminating in a huge stone-lined pool. The original pavilion which faced it has been replaced by a modern structure. This large man-made pool is repeated in another garden on a very much grander scale at a place called Shah Gul, supposedly originally built in 1785 by an unknown king, although it was further developed in the nineteenth century to its present state with terraces and a pavilion.

This lake garden is similar to that of the Bagh-i Takht at Shiraz, and the form must represent the full flowering of the development of Persian garden design, before the advent of twentieth-century gardens on a smaller scale with, sadly, Western horticultural influences. The vast pool of Shah Gul was not excavated from a level site, but was built up on its north side with great earth banks which were then planted. As in the garden in Shiraz, natural water feeds this lake, progressing across a series of terraces in five streams, making as many waterfalls at each level and finally ending in the lake which hangs suspended above the valley beyond. The rest of the garden area between the terraces is divided into plots planted with fruit trees. A major feature of this garden is a causeway which runs into the lake and on which sits a pleasure pavilion, surrounded by water. The

OPPOSITE *The entrance to an inner courtyard of the shrine of Sayyid Shah Nimatullah at Kerman, Iran, with the domed building that houses the tomb in the background.*

*An 1840 engraving of the reception hall of the Gulistan Palace
in Tehran, built by the Qajar ruler, Fath Ali Shah, and completed by 1806.
A throne is situated in the* talar *of a typical reception pavilion,
which looks onto a paved courtyard and central pool.*

central hall of the pavilion is octagonal in shape, some twelve metres across, and was originally crowned with a dome. Corner angles of the pavilion are broken up into a series of small chambers.

When Fath Ali Shah, the nephew of Aga Muhammad Khan, moved to Tehran in 1788, construction started in earnest, with new gardens, palaces, public squares, government buildings and private houses. Of the many palaces that Fath Ali Shah and his court built few remain, and even fewer are worthy of comment in this context. However, the Gulistan palace does remain, with its gem-studded thrones. It was completed in 1806, and at its inception was yet another series of pavilions, albeit exceedingly grand ones for dazzling formal receptions, all within a garden layout. Traditional buildings, with *talar*, were combined with more Western forms, for Tehran, being 900 metres above sea level, was therefore considerably colder during some parts of the year than some other regal locations. The garden of the

Gulistan was in fact quite small, no more than an acre and, according to an early account, was bright with tulips, narcissi and anemones, sown as if by chance on a green lawn.

The favourite residence of Fath Ali Shah was the Negaristan. Its pavilions were completed in 1810, set within a garden of several acres. The entrance portal was on the long axis which led to a tall octagonal structure known as the Kula Ferangi, or European Hat. This was situated at the centre of the garden and approached between an arcade of trees, all full-grown and luxuriant, whose trunks were covered by a rich undergrowth of roses, lilacs and other fragrant and aromatic shrubs. The feature of this structure was a large pool and playing fountain, set in the centre of the main room. At the far end of the axial avenue was the circular building known as the Negaristan. Robert Ker Porter, an early nineteenth-century diarist and traveller, wrote of it: 'At the upper end of the garden is a small and fantastically built palace, enclosed in a little paradise of sweets. The Shah often retires there for days together, at the beginning of summer . . . and accompanied by the softer sex of his family, forgets, for a while, that life or the world have other seasons than the gay and lovely spring.'

Yet another pavilion which caught the eye of European diarists was that of the summer bath, known as the Taj-i Dowlat, or Crown of the Kingdom. This structure was at least two storeys high, with the upper floor taken up by apartments for women. Below was the marble bath, with a long marble slide serving as a means to enter it from above. Ker Porter said that it was

filled with clearest water sparkling in the sun, for its only canopy is the vault of heaven; but rose trees with other pendant shrubs bearing flowers cluster near it; and at times their waving branches throw a beautifully quivering shade over the excessive brightness of the water. The royal master takes his noonday repose in one of the upper chambers which encircle the saloon of the bath, and if he be inclined he has only to turn his eyes to the scene below, to see the loveliest objects of his tenderness, sporting like naiads amidst the crystal stream and glowing with all the bloom and brilliancy which belong to Asiatic youth.

Speaking of the rose trees, which grew to twenty feet in height with a trunk two feet in circumference and which were so smothered in flowers of the English hedge-rose type that they concealed the trunk, Ker Porter goes on to report: 'in no country of the world does the rose grow in such perfection as in Persia; in no country is it so cultivated, and prized by the

natives. Their gardens and courts are crowded with its plants, their rooms ornamented with vases, filled with its gathered bunches and every bath strewn with the full blown flowers, plucked from their ever replenished stems.'

Other palaces, which continued to be built by successive Qajar rulers throughout the nineteenth century, were located north of Tehran in the foothills of the Alborz mountain range, in the area now known as Shemiran. This favoured location was considerably cooler than the city below, with cool mountain breezes and ever-present rushing water. Little now remains of these gardens, and their acres have been covered with housing, as smart Tehran creeps northwards.

Approached by a wide avenue from the desert town of Kashan is the royal garden, Bagh-i Fin. It is the only surviving garden of historical merit in Iran, and therefore worthy of closer examination. Donald Wilber says that the site was used to honour the Safavid ruler Shah Ismail in 1504, and that later, in 1587, Shah Abbas I erected structures on the site and presumably built the garden, so it is contemporary with the best Mughal gardens; it was certainly there when visited by Shah Abbas II in 1659. After this the buildings vanished, and were re-erected by Fath Ali Shah

ABOVE *An 1867 engraving of the Qasr-i Qajar, or Castle of the Qajars, also built by Fath Ali Shah (reigned 1799–1834) and one of the largest of the many Qajar palaces in the hilly Shemiran region north of Tehran. A European influence is beginning to appear in both the structure and layout of the garden.*

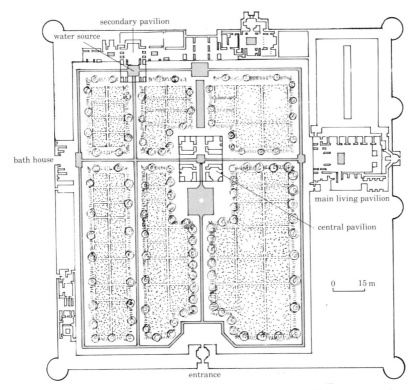

water source
secondary pavilion
bath house
main living pavilion
central pavilion
entrance

0   15 m

ABOVE *Plan of the Bagh-i Fin at Kashan in central Iran, which was restored by Fath Ali Shah between 1799 and 1834. It is one of the most complete quadripartite gardens extant in Iran.*

BELOW *A corner of the Bagh-i Fin showing a typical brimming pool and water channels with fountains.*

*Edged with stone and lined with blue faience tiles, the water channels
in the Bagh-i Fin are constantly alive with the sound of bubbling water.*

between 1799 and 1834, the years of his rule. The format of the garden probably remained, and it was restored along with the buildings by Fath Ali. Persians know the garden as the place where Amir-i Kabir, a prime minister of Fath Ali, was murdered in the baths adjacent to the garden, and certainly after the incident the gardens again went into a decline, until they were once more restored in 1935 when the Bagh-i Fin was named a national monument of Iran.

The central pavilion of the garden is still under repair, although considerable work has been completed in the surrounding buildings to the garden. The interest of the Bagh-i Fin is that it is a modified version of the *chahar bagh*, with a primary water axis from the entrance, through the central pavilion, to another at the top of the garden, and the whole plan falls gently from the north to the south with a cross-axis bisecting this. The layout is slightly unusual in that a secondary main axis cuts the left-hand part of the garden, but is justified by virtue of the fact that the water source is introduced into the garden in a square pool at the south end of it. This pool, like all the canals bisecting the garden, is lined with blue faience tiles, and water welling up in it is reflected in the arched roof of a charming little pavilion which stands above it. All the watercourses are then connected by one perimeter course before the flow runs out into the village beyond, going first to a watermill, then into a pretty little tea garden, and so on. Within the skeleton of the watercourses, the main garden is further cut up by raised walks, bordered by massive cypress trees. Fruit trees are then planted in the areas bordered by cypresses, although one cannot imagine that they are particularly productive beneath their shade.

Many of the watercourses have small bubbling fountains welling up within them and are slightly reminiscent of the Mughal versions; however, the garden is not on such a grand scale. Indeed the charm of the Bagh-i Fin lies in its comparatively small size, combined with a certain rusticity. Some parts of the outer watercourse, for instance, are planted with willows, with yellow flowering cannas between them; ducks paddle about in their shade. The overpowering sensation of the garden is of light and shade, accompanied by the constant rush and gurgle of water and the deep, evocative, resinous scent of the cypresses warmed by the sun. The Baghi-Fin is enclosed by high cargill walls (a mixture of mud and straw) and it stands out from its desert surround, for the colony of tall sentinel cypresses

it encloses seems alien against the stark mountain backdrop. They do emphasize, however, the contrast between the aridity outside and the lush calm within.

Exploring the water source of the garden outside the walls is a worthwhile exercise, for much thought has gone into its control. On the north side of the garden, beyond its surrounding road, there is quite a complex of buildings to take the water from its underground channel from the mountain and filter and direct it on its various ways. The water is first collected in a cool clear pool with a pavilion at one end, and there are steps down into it on either side. This, one may surmise, was an ablutionary

ABOVE *The water from the Bagh-i Fin runs into a public tea garden,*
where wooden frames covered with carpets or cushions
are placed over the canal so that the maximum coolness
can be enjoyed from the water rushing beneath.

bath pool for staff from the household. From this bath the water is filtered into a second shallow pool – perhaps for washing clothes – and then the course is divided. One feed runs into the garden itself, while the other is taken down the east side of the garden in a raised channel to feed the bath houses which are on that side of the layout. The course has now been broken, but the channels still exist and the water now feeds the surrounding village houses.

About a mile to the south, above the garden at the foot of the mountain, is a little terraced layout with fields and orchards. This receives water from a reservoir tank high above it, which it then feeds on to the main garden at Fin. Was this perhaps the farm providing fruit and vegetables to the household? The order and layout seem too organized to be incidental and a peasant farmer would certainly not be allowed water before the shah. A very narrow water channel, covered by only a few inches of earth and supporting grass above it, feeds the top reservoir tank, and this green band snakes high up into the mountains through the arid rocky desert. Below the Bagh-i Fin to the north and on either side of Kashan, the ground is well watered with high-walled orchards and small fields of corn. The ground then levels out to the great salt desert of the Dasht-i Kavir beyond, which with the Dasht-e Lut occupies the whole of central Iran.

Outside the southern city of Kerman at Mahan, at a height of 6,000 feet and set in a green valley, flanked by snow-capped mountains in a setting of incomparable clarity and peace, is the tomb of Sayyid Shah Nimatullah, a Sufi savant and poet. Sir Roger Stevens, the Persian art historian, describes the tomb as comprising 'the most ravishing single group of buildings in Iran'. The earliest of them date back to some time after 1431, the year of the death of the mystic in whose memory they were built; however, the tomb itself was enlarged and beautified during the reign of Shah Abbas I, with later Qajar additions in the 1840s. This collection of buildings sounds rather a muddle, but they fit together remarkably well. From our point of view, it is the garden enclosures which they surround that are of importance, and it is they which make this complex into a true paradise, with its atmosphere of tranquillity and seclusion. Above the central pool in the main courtyard, surrounded by eight majestic cypresses and eight umbrella pines, the brilliant blue of the Safavid dome flashes in the sun.

The complex contains a progression of courtyards on a central axis; the

first, when approached from the eastern side, is large and open, with a central rectangular pool mirroring the blue sky. The buildings surrounding it are set back and lined with recesses in which pilgrims to the tomb rest on carpets. From this courtyard one progresses into the central one, in the centre of which is a cruciform-shaped tank with a central octagonal basin. From it comes the merest ripple of water. Round the tank are banked rows of gay geraniums, their brilliant colouring of red and orange contrasting with the strong yellow, blue and pink of the boisterous tilework on the walls around, and the whole lightly canopied over by the pine trees. The plan is simplicity itself; it is the combination of building, water and planting which adds up to such a glorious entity in the clear sunlight. Beyond the central tomb chamber a smaller courtyard has an old apple tree leaning across a small pool, flanked by four guardian cypresses – in direct contrast to the previous court which is terminated by a central

ABOVE *Part of the cruciform tank in the inner courtyard
of the shrine of Sayyid Shah Nimatullah at Kerman
in southern central Iran. Shaded by cypress trees and umbrella pines,
the pool is ringed by pots of brilliant coloured geraniums.*

114

Safavid *ivan* with two magnificent Qajar minarets.

As if one were not already sated with beauty at Mahan, a few kilometres outside the village and running up into the mountains is the nineteenth-century garden of Firuz Mirza, the son of Muhammad Shah, known as the garden of Farman Farma. Work is still continuing on the restoration of this garden which is strongly reminsicent of Kashmiri gardens and the later Shirazi layouts. Broadly, the plan is of a pavilion complex at either end of an ascending pool, flanked by beds on either side, within an avenue of cypresses. Beyond these are the fruit orchards. The top complex of buildings was residential, with a view down the terraced water levels to an extraordinary open pavilion at the bottom. The remoteness of this garden, and the mood it evokes (probably even more because of its decaying state), is magical and a wonderful example of later Qajar Persian layout.

ABOVE *The nineteenth-century garden of Farman Farma outside Mahan, Iran.*
A residential pavilion at the top of the garden
looks down a central staircase of water to a remarkable open gateway
at the bottom, with mountains rising behind.

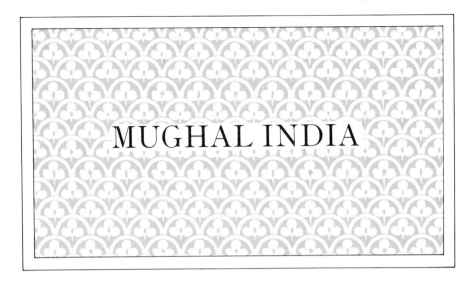

MUGHAL INDIA

The garden tradition which Babur, the first great Mughal, was to carry to the hot dusty plains of northern India is purely Persian in concept, enclosed, private and quadripartite – the *chahar bagh*. But over the next two centuries his descendants with their passion for garden building took this Persian form and transformed it into another which is unique in the garden tradition worldwide.

The Muslim world possesses the particular skill of imbuing an Islamic idea with the local flavour, be it in poetry, in art or in building. In the latter half of the sixteenth century and the early part of the seventeenth, this genius reached one of its finest flowerings in Mughal gardens in India, mainly centred on Kashmir, for the gardens of Agra, Lahore and Delhi, being out of the hill country, were closed and private, albeit with views to the outside world, in the continuing Persian tradition. This recurring influence from Persia can be traced back to pre-Timurid times, for all the central Asian invaders (from Alexander onwards) had passed through, inevitably bringing some echoes of Persian culture with them. (Even the word 'Hindu' is Persian, simply meaning Indian.)

What was the previous tradition onto which that of Timurid Persia was so successfully grafted? Until 1200 when Muslims united the region – at least in the north-west – India had been a series of minor Hindu states and kingdoms, each going its own way, ruled by individual families or clans. Since the eighth century the north-west had been increasingly dominated by the Rajput dynasties, which professed Hinduism as did all

OPPOSITE *A Mughal miniature of c. 1610–1615 showing friends in a garden. Despite the Indian setting, the formal division of the garden and its use as a kind of extended living area are characteristic of the Persian* chahar bagh.

Indians in that part of the country. Hinduism is both a way of life and a highly organized social and religious system, but free from any dogma concerning the nature of God. It does not depend on the existence or non-existence of God, or whether there is one God or many – this is not ultimately what matters. What does is the eternal law that governs all human and non-human existence, which the Western world understands as 'natural law'. It is the subtlety and ambivalence in the interpretation of this concept which gives Hinduism its distinctive flavour and which sets up within it a tension that is never wholly resolved.

Apart from the fact that the Islamic movement was a relatively recent graft on the ancient and firmly established social and religious structure of India, it also clashed head on with its fundamental convictions. Islam promoted realism against Hindu idealism, the material against the visionary and the concrete against the abstract. Nothing could illustrate this religious and racial difference, or emphasize more clearly the principles underlying the consciousness of each community, than the contrast between their respective places of worship. Compared with the clarity of the mosque, the temple is a place of mystery; the courts of the Muslim are open to air and light, the Hindu temple is a building of enclosure, of sombre passages leading to dim cells, guarded and remote. The mosque has no need of a central shrine, it is sufficient to turn in the direction of Mecca; but the focal point of the temple is a sacred chamber within the labyrinth of the building. The mosque is wholly visible and intelligible, while the temple is complex and indeterminate.

Islamic art was the very antithesis of Hindu art; for Hindu adornment was individualistic, irregular and symbiotic, while Islamic decoration was mathematical, continuous and abstract. Hindu art employed writing only as an inferior method of supplying information, while Islamic art used it as one of its principal means of expression and indeed as the vehicle of God's word. Islamic monotheism, too, was at odds with the quixotic complexities of Hindu religion, and many Hindus found this an attractive alternative and a way of escape from the intolerable degradations of the caste system for the outcasts and untouchables.

The fusion of these different ideological conceptions of Indo-Islamic art, religion and thinking was the basis of Mughal design; while their basic philosophy was Muslim, its manifestation in building and garden was often carried out by Hindu craftsmen, so that the blending of concept and actuality produced a result far less rigid than that of the parent Persian tradition, though none-the-less brilliant in its own right. Indian craftsmen were unequalled in their skill and knowledge in using stone, having achieved perfection by working it for centuries in temple buildings; its manipulation was practised on a scale which raised it to the status of a national industry. How this manipulative skill was adapted and directed to the production of technically as well as artistically accomplished architecture is seen in the monuments that arose in India under Islamic rule.

Until this time Indian building construction had been fairly primitive and involved no structural complexities. The true arch was not known, the beam being used to span voids, together with the constructional method known as corbelling. The displacement of the beam by the arch, evolved under Muslim influence, was made possible by the introduction of another material, hitherto unknown to the indigenous masons: this was a cementing agent in the form of mortar. With this the effects of oblique and lateral thrust could be counteracted, and far greater flexibility was possible to put into practice the scientific and mechanical formulae which Islam had evolved in its own particular building forms.

While the mosque was the most important building of Islam, the tomb was also introduced, as an entirely new kind of structure, since in Hindu India at that time no sepulchre was raised to mark the resting place of the dead. In the course of time, though, tomb building, especially in northern India, became part of the landscape, with much of the finest Indo-Islamic design coming together in their structures, and with the concept of the *chahar bagh* evolving in a new form to surround them.

The topography of northern India had to be considered as well, and particularly that of Kashmir. In the Perso-Arab tradition of building in a desert environment, every last drop of water was of physical as well as visual value, heightened by the privacy of the shaded gardens in which it was enjoyed. Away from the hot plains of India, in the cool Vale of Kashmir, water was not at a premium; there were rushing mountain streams and lakes to delight the Mughal emperors. Indeed, flat land suitable for garden building was scarce, as the mountains dropped rapidly into the lake, and ground levels and contours had to be exploited by terracing. Water remained the unifying theme in both situations: its use in the narrow channels of the flat, quartered gardens of Persia was translated into ever-increasing, rushing water displays of greater com-

OVERLEAF *Two Mughal miniatures of 1663, showing on the right Shah Jahan seated on a terrace with his son Dara Shikuh and chief minister Asaf Khan, and on the left a group of courtiers. Behind Shah Jahan a canal flows through a pavilion and on past bed-rolls at the water's edge before cascading below the terrace. The left-hand miniature reveals more of the formal divisions and planting of the garden. With hills in the distance (some snow-covered), the pictures probably represent the Shalamar Bagh in Kashmir.*

plexity in India, and it was this tradition which was later transferred back to the water gardens first of the Zands and then of the Qajars in Persia.

One cannot but compare the revelation which the early Renaissance gardens of Italy must have been to the northern European on the Grand Tour, after the enclosed medieval gardens of Europe (based, it is supposed, on those of Islamic Spain), with that of the Mughal seeing Kashmir for the first time. Of course, the basic intention behind the European garden tradition is quite different, but a comparison may be drawn between the Italian Renaissance garden with its fearless acceptance of, and ultimate marriage to, surrounding nature, and the open terraced layouts of Mughal gardens in Kashmir, with which they are contemporary. Indo-Islamic art before the coming of the Mughals already showed certain Muslim Persian elements; their proximity made this inevitable. Though based on this earlier Indo-Islamic fusion, the buildings of the earlier Mughal garden palaces derived their unique flavour from the combination of subtle-toned red and yellow local stone – a departure from clear-cut Persian colours – with Hindu motifs in such details as lintels, columns and eaves, fretted balconies or lotus roundels, while carving was rich with flowers and animals, flower scrolls being combined with Muslim inscriptions. Akbar later (1572–3) conquered Gujarat, famed for its white marble, and increasingly this was used for building. Not until the sixteenth century did the new and original Indo-Muslim art of the great Mughals reach its full flowering, since the Emperors Babur and Humayun were too involved with martial pursuits. Akbar, however, set up his court in a very eclectic fashion, once peace had been established with the Rajput princes; in it were mingled Mughal, Indo-Islamic and Rajput elements. This fusing of styles continued through the reign of Jahangir, but the greatest builder of all was Shah Jahan.

So the Mughal style developed, a combination of arches, pilasters, perforated marble screens, pavilions decorated with arabesques, inscriptions, flowers in relief or inlay, and semi-precious stones of turquoise, purple and blue, of fountains and canals in an expanded form of the traditional *chahar bagh*; and this style came from several sources: a previous Indo-Muslim philosophy, the curving architecture of Bengal, the white marble of Gujarat and the floral decoration of Kashmir. This refinement culminated in the Taj Mahal at Agra and should have expanded by incorporating new ideas and inspiration, but was prevented by Aurang-

zeb's intensification of orthodox Muslim policy; art and architecture started its slow decline and deterioration to the needlessly intricate and over-ornate decadence of the later Mughals, even returning eventually to the predominant use of red sandstone in the buildings of the Raj.

The reign of the Mughals was well documented, primarily by the emperors themselves in the *Baburnama, Humayunnama, Akbarnama,* and

ABOVE *A sixteenth-century Mughal miniature of Akbar and his court in a walled garden. Where there was no natural slope, water wheels were used to pump the water round the garden.*

the *Tuzuk-i Jahangir*, or Memoirs of Jahangir. Secondary observations came from visiting ambassadors and travellers from the West. These written accounts were supplemented by court drawings and miniatures, so that a total picture of the developing glitter of the Mughal court and its decline is available, and with it a vivid description of court life and the gardens in which it was often lived.

Unlike other dynasties whose current ruler built only for himself in his own lifetime – for a new ruler needed a new palace if not a new capital – the Mughals, while sometimes building afresh, also extended royal building complexes they had inherited, so that they tended not to fall away to oblivion. Added to this, the Mughals followed the Timurid tradition of building tombs for themselves, surrounding them with a garden which was enjoyed during their lifetime and which at their death became their last revered resting place (though this Muslim tradition was existing in northern India before their arrival). We have therefore, in a better or worse state of repair, a far greater number of gardens built in an order which can be analysed chronologically than anywhere else in Islam. This, combined with the Mughal tradition of building first in readily available stone and later in marble, has ensured that tomb or palace and garden have all survived.

BABUR (1483–1530)

Babur was born in 1483. His father was Umar Shaikh, ruler of a minor state called Ferghana in Transoxiana, bordering Samarkand, one of many small states that sprang up after the death of Timur, and all ruled by his descendants who constantly wrangled and fought among themselves for superiority, not unlike the Taifa kings of al-Andalus. The strongest of these states was Samarkand itself, Timur's old, rich and fabled capital, along with Bukhara and, further south, Herat in what is now Afghanistan. Quite early in his career Babur set his sights on capturing Samarkand, and in 1496 he attacked it with two cousins, at a time when Samarkand itself was weakened by the death in quick successsion of two of its rulers. They were in fact beaten off, but returned the following year and, after a seven-month siege, entered the city. Babur had obviously heard of the riches of Timur's famed city, and eagerly explored them, being particularly taken by the gardens which he described in his *Baburnama*.

But Babur's success only lasted a few months, then he was deserted by many of his followers and lost the city, only to discover that in his absence he had also lost his own kingdom of Ferghana to his younger brother, Jahangir, in the meantime. Babur set about recapturing his kingdom and by 1500 he had made a treaty with his brother whereby each agreed to rule half of the country, and further that they should jointly attack Samarkand once more, Jahangir keeping the whole of Ferghana if the offensive was successful. Initially they enjoyed success, but by 1504 Babur was under attack from the Uzbek Shaibani Khan, who eventually squeezed him out of Ferghana, and for the second time Babur was homeless.

Babur now set his sights on Kabul, three hundred miles to the south, which was being ruled from Kandahar by a non-Timurid prince. He took it easily. At Kabul – a crossroads of the Islamic trading world between trading routes stretching east, west, north and south – for the first time in his life Babur was able to lead a settled existence, and quickly set up court. Kabul is situated in a green and fertile valley, and the court which Babur established, if not achieving the cultural standards of the court at Samarkand, was not far behind. In this settled haven Babur was able to indulge himself in writing poetry and starting his first garden building. His favourite was the Bagh-i Vafa, which he describes in his memoirs:

> I laid out the four gardens, known as Bagh-i Vafa, on a rising ground facing south. . . . There oranges, citrons and pomegranates grow in abundance . . . I had plantains brought and planted there; they did very well. The year before I had had sugar cane planted there; it also did well. . . . The garden lies high, has running water close at hand, and a mild winter climate. In the middle of it a one-mill stream flows constantly past the little hill on which are the four garden plots. In the south-west part there is a reservoir ten by ten, round which are orange trees, and a few pomegranates, the whole encircled by a trefoil meadow. This is the best part of the garden, a most beautiful sight when the oranges take colour. Truly that garden is admirably sited.

Later in his life, when apparently settled in India, Babur still thought of Kabul and found time to write to its governor with instructions that the gardens he had planted should be kept well-watered and properly maintained with flowers.

درختهای انار هم هست کرد و حوض تمام سه بر که ز آر

جای این باغ همین است در وقت زرد شدن بار بسیار

Babur's court became a sanctuary for other dispossessed Timurid princes who had lost their kingdoms as Shaibani Khan extended his. Even Babur began to grow uneasy when Shaibani took Herat, but at this stage the latter fell foul of Shah Ismail, the founder of the Persian Safavid dynasty, who eventually captured and beheaded him. The shah returned Shaibani's widow, Babur's sister Khanzada, to him. This gesture marks Babur's first direct communication with Persia, although culturally there must already have been a strong interchange. The relationship developed to the point where the shah promised to help Babur retake Samarkand on the condition that Babur adopt the dress and customs of the shah's Persian Shii sect of Islam. Shah Ismail obviously saw this as a way to expand his boundaries; Babur was prepared to accept the shah's conditions as he was still allowed to practise his own Sunni form of Islam in Kabul. Babur duly marched north, first taking Bukhara from the Uzbeks and, as a Timurid prince returning to his rightful possession, took Samarkand too, while tactfully keeping his Persian allies in the background.

Again his success was not to endure since Babur found himself in the ambiguous position of seemingly having to persecute Samarkand's Sunni population while wearing the guise of Ismail's Shii doctrine. The residents of Samarkand soon grew tired of Babur and he was rejected from the city after eight months, when it was returned to the Uzbeks. Babur returned to his haven of Kabul.

Before his last, ill-fated attempt on Samarkand, Babur had made one or two assaults eastwards into India, if for no other reason than to make foraging raids to provide for his by now huge court, which his little green valley in Kabul could not support. Like Samarkand, Babur still saw Hindustan, and more particularly the Punjab, as his by right, his claim going back to Timur's conquest of northern India in 1398. Timur had left as his vassal in control of Delhi a man called Khizr Khan, who later became Sultan of Delhi and founded the Sayyid dynasty while he still owed allegiance to the Timurids. His successor at the time of Babur's invasion was the Lodi Sultan Ibrahim II of Delhi.

Babur took his time in preparing his offensive into India. Kandahar fell to him in 1522 and he was then free to turn his attention to India, and successive yearly raids were made until Babur defeated Sultan Ibrahim at the battle of Panipat in 1526, aided by the abilities of his seventeen-year-old son Humayun and newly imported firearms from Turkey. It is

OPPOSITE *In this Mughal miniature of c. 1590 Babur is shown supervising*
the layout of the Bagh-i Vafa at Kabul in 1504,
which, with its enclosing wall (here supporting pomegranates),
quadripartite division by water channels, and water tank, displays
all the typical features of the traditional Islamic garden.

recorded that at Panipat he built a garden to celebrate a victory – and a tomb for Ibrahim. His victory at Panipat marked the end of the Delhi Sultanate and established in its place the Mughal empire. After this victory Humayun was dispatched to the capital Agra, to take the fort and its treasure, while Babur marched on Delhi, which he took, proclaiming himself Emperor of Hindustan. Previous Muslim sultans, beginning with the Slave Kings in 1206, had placed their capital in Delhi. Lahore had been the capital of Ghaznavid India since the mid-eleventh century and was roughly the area we now know as Pakistan, and it also fell. The spread southward of Islam took longer, and the taking of the Deccan was a continual Mughal operation, not completed until the reign of Akbar (1556–1605), the grandson of Babur. It is from this time also that Islam spread rapidly eastward into Malaya, Java and Borneo in South-East Asia.

Babur spent the rest of his life campaigning; remarkably, however, he took an active interest in all that he saw while doing so and kept a rough diary which was later to be transposed into his impressions, the *Baburnama*, and which gave an extremely full picture of sixteenth-century Hindustan. He also continued his garden building, for he and his followers found the lack of water, the dust and the heat of India exceedingly tiresome after green Kabul. 'One of the great defects of Hindustan', Babur writes, 'being its lack of running waters, it kept coming to my mind that waters should be made to flow by means of wheels erected wherever I might settle down, also that grounds should be laid out in an orderly and symmetrical way.'

It is not certain which is the site of the first garden which he built at Agra. It seems evidence exists that he built a garden palace at the bend of the river looking south across it, and that this was later completed by his son, Humayun. Traditionally this has been known as the *Chahar Bagh*, and traces of a number of wells and buildings have been found. The greater probability, however, is that the real site is that of the Ram Bagh, originally the Aram Bagh, or Garden of Rest. It is almost certainly the earliest Mughal garden to survive in recognizable form, although much altered since. It too could be described as orderly and symmetrical, as Babur wished. The basic pattern is one of geometrically laid-out walks, with platforms, from which the garden can be viewed, raised well above ground level. Possibly it was in this newly constructed garden that Babur received all the descendants of Timur and Jenghiz Khan, and all who had

ABOVE LEFT *The Ram Bagh, Agra, built in 1526, is one of the earliest surviving Mughal gardens. Situated on the other side of the River Jumna to the Red Fort, the garden has the kind of orderly and symmetrical layout that Babur would have favoured.*

ABOVE RIGHT *A sixteenth-century Mughal miniature showing Babur receiving envoys in his garden at Agra. With the Red Fort perhaps in the background, this may well represent the Ram Bagh.*

served him in the past, bidden in 1528 'to receive fitting benefits' for their support, and to celebrate Babur's undoubted supremacy. At this magnificent feast, guests sat in a semi-circle stretching a hundred metres, with Babur at the centre in a pavilion erected for the occasion. The main attractions of feasting and the giving of presents were accompanied by animal fights, wrestling, dancing and acrobatics – very similar in fact to the receptions given first by Timur, then by Shah Abbas whom Babur preceded by comparatively few years. The Ram Bagh was well maintained in his great-grandson Jahangir's reign since he wrote of it in glowing terms.

Babur died in 1530, a comparatively young man, his death hastened by excessive alcohol and opium – but he had achieved an enormous amount in his remarkable career. He was first buried in a garden on the bank of the river Jumna at Agra, but his wish was to be buried in his favourite garden in Kabul, which he always referred to as home and where he was finally taken.

HUMAYUN (1508–56)

Babur had died within four years of seizing Hindustan and founding the Mughal dynasty, so that the inheritance which he left to his son Humayun in 1530 was little more than a military occupation which had been held together by his own indomitable spirit. Combined with this state of insecurity, Humayun was further troubled by his three brothers who, in the Timurid tradition, had each inherited part of the kingdom on their father's death, but who continued to try to expand that inheritance at Humayun's expense. His life was therefore one of constant fighting, compounded by the ever-present intrusions of Sher (later Shah) Khan, the leader of the many Afghans who over the years had settled along the Ganges in Bihar and who constantly threatened to overrun Bengal.

Within ten years of coming to the throne of Babur's empire, Humayun had lost most of it and was forced to flee towards Persia, where he was received, entertained and finally helped by Shah Tahmasp, the grandfather of the great Shah Abbas. On his way to Persia, however, Humayun visited Herat and Mashhad and was eventually received in northern Persia at Qazvin. This journey no doubt brought home to Humayun the Timurid cultural traditions to which he was heir, and especially the one associated with him in particular: that of miniature painting, for he alone of all the early great Mughals was not particularly interested in the art of garden making. Shah Tahmasp supported Humayun in attacking the Indian territories belonging to his brother Kamran on the promise of Kandahar

OPPOSITE *The tomb of Humayun in Delhi, with its Persian-influenced central ivan, was completed in 1573. The central watercourse is quite small, since water would be at a premium.*

being given to him on its capture. The shah's young son Murad was to accompany Humayun and would become his father's representative in the captured city. Kandahar fell to the advancing Humayun, aided by the shah's 12,000 horsemen, and was duly given to the Persians in 1545. The young Murad soon died, however, and Humayun took over the city; from here he then retook Kabul as well.

Over the next eight years Humayun slowly advanced, finally taking Delhi again in 1555 and remounting his father's throne. For the remaining settled year of his life, Humayun's court was one of great culture, especially of painting and poetry. While Humayun was not a soldier of his father's standing, he was something of a sybarite, who, even in his most troubled times politically, would retire into his harem for days or weeks, smoking opium to which he too was addicted.

Humayun's widow, Hamida Begum, a Persian from Khurasan, supervised the construction of his tomb in Delhi, which was begun around 1560

and completed in 1573. It was to be the first of a succession of monumental garden tombs built by the Mughals. It stands on a large square platform and rises high with an immense marble dome which indicates its Persian origins.

The tomb sits in the only extant Mughal garden to preserve its original form. This form is purely Persian too, although the *chahar bagh* layout has become enlarged and more intricate to become a water parterre of narrow channels with shallow tanks at their intersections.

AKBAR (1542–1605)

Akbar came to the throne in 1556 when still young; he was crowned at the age of thirteen, in a garden in Kalanaur. His guardian, wisely appointed before his death by Humayun, was Barram Khan. During his long life, the great Akbar not only expanded the borders of Muslim India, but turned what had been virtually a military state into one controlled amazingly efficiently by a civil service. He had the good sense to repeal laws and taxes against the infidel Hindu and other minorities, and tried to assimilate their civilization into Mughal Islam, not without opposition within his own camp. To this end also, Akbar married a Rajput princess, the daughter of the Rajah of Amber (now Jaipur) in 1562; later she became the mother of the next emperor Jahangir, who in turn married a Rajput princess, thus binding the Mughals with the most important and powerful Hindu princes in northern India, Rajputana and Rajasthan. Akbar also made a point of taking other Rajput princesses into his household. Towards the end of his life it became feared that he had in fact become Hindu himself – he dabbled with Christianity also – but he had become neither, although he did display a great interest in mystical Sufism.

In his early years Akbar and his court were constantly on the move, taking vast armies with him under the guise of hunting parties, which served the secondary purpose of keeping any opposition subdued. In fact he was extremely fond of hunting from an early age, being very much the outdoor type rather than the scholar. His tutors despaired of his cultural abilities, and it is assumed that he could neither read nor write throughout his long life. The type of hunting most favoured by the Mughals was to drive game into an ever-decreasing circle surrounded by beaters, and only when that circle was a few miles across did the emperor go in to the kill with his favourite cheetahs or Indian leopards, and after him came lesser members of his household. But the initial diameter of the beaters' circle might have been a hundred kilometres, needing up to fifty thousand men to enclose it. Such an operation was indeed a military exercise, and both Jenghiz Khan and Timur before Akbar had favoured this type of hunt for its value as military training. By this technique of moving his armies about, Akbar – between inevitable clashes – had by 1570 obtained recognition of his sovereignty from nearly all the prominent Hindu princes; but the twenty-six-year-old emperor still had no heir, despite his ample supply of wives. It had always been Akbar's habit to visit holy men from time to time to enlist their prayers to this end. After one such visit to Shaikh Salim Chishti, who was living at Sikri, and having been told that he would have three male heirs, he found that his wife, the former Princess of Amber, was indeed pregnant. Her son, born in 1569, was christened Salim after the sage, but later he became the Emperor Jahangir. Two other sons followed, Murad in 1570 and Danyal in 1572. To celebrate the birth of his heir, Akbar decided to move his capital from Agra and build a new one at Sikri, to be known as *Fathpur Sikri* ('fathpur' denoting victory).

At Agra Akbar had started building the magnificent red sandstone wall twenty metres high which encloses and gives its name to the Red Fort there. The wall runs in the shape of a bow, with the straight side facing the river Jumna, on to which so much later Mughal building also faced. Along the top of this wall Akbar had built his palace, although all that now remains of it is the Jahangiri Mahal, the rest having been demolished by Shah Jahan for his more refined marble buildings.

From Agra it is an hour's journey to Fathpur Sikri, which is now something of a ghost town, for Akbar lived in it no longer than fourteen years before it was abandoned. What remains in a state of restoration is the complex of palace and garden buildings on which thousands of craftsmen started to work in 1571, building in a totally Indian style. Later Mughal architecture combined considerable Persian influences. At both Agra and Fathpur Sikri we know that Akbar had gardens built, importing trees and flowers of all kinds. But architecture was Akbar's chief interest, not gardens. The mosque courtyard is magnificent, the huge *ivan* entrance of red sandstone with marble inlay being reminiscent of Persian architecture in its scale. Sitting in the middle of the courtyard and contrasting with its surroundings is the marble tomb which Shah Jahan built for Shaikh Salim Chishti, whose prayers Akbar sought to bless him with a family. This little tomb building is again of exquisite refinement, and much in its design is in the Indian tradition. Outside, a deserted ablution pool, empty of water, sits in the mosque courtyard, which nevertheless has the feeling of a market place. Here it becomes so hot that mats are laid to walk on barefoot for as it is a holy place one goes shoeless. The flooring of the mosque court is of stone and therefore hot, while marble remains cool.

A little way from the mosque is Akbar's private palace, built entirely of red sandstone in the Indian style and of perfectly tailored slabs which in general only rest on each other. Again, this is a strangely gloomy building because of its colour. What is interesting is the use of coursed water channels throughout the complex and the huge regular *chaman* tank in the main courtyard, with its central island and bridges leading to it, surely one of the earliest of this form of island retreat. Akbar's Fathpur Sikri illustrates clearly not only the scattered nature of the palace pavilions

The tomb of Shaikh Salim Chisti, the only marble building in Akbar's red sandstone palace at Fathpur Sikri outside Agra, which was built in a predominantly Indian style from 1571.

but the openness of their design, intended to catch every cooling breeze; remarkable, too, is the lack of surround or balustrading to floors of considerable height – for, if one sits cross-legged on the ground, one wants an unimpeded view.

Various reasons have been put forward for the desertion of Fathpur Sikri: that the situation was unhealthy or the supply of water was inadequate. It is said that the dam of the lake actually gave way while the emperor and his friends were playing cards on the bank and the party narrowly escaped drowning. For whatever reason, Akbar moved his court to the Punjab in 1585, and from there he started to make visits to Kashmir – which for us is significant – and on his return in 1598 he moved to Agra. This whole period of Akbar's life has been faithfully recorded in two works by the Persian Abu l-Fazl, the *Akbarnama* and the *Ayn-i Akbari*, or 'Regulations of Akbar', and it was this recorded, ordered existence of court life and the wide administrative apparatus surrounding it which became the life and culture of succeeding Mughal courts over the next hundred years.

Akbar's first visit to Kashmir after its conquest in 1586 was a revelation to him – he fell in love with it – even despite the journey, for which he had three thousand stone cutters, mountain miners and splitters of rock and two thousand diggers to level the ups and downs of the roadway. On

ABOVE *The main courtyard and tank with its central platform and bridges in Akbar's private palace at Fathpur Sikri.*

this first visit, river palaces, floating gardens and over a thousand boats were prepared in his honour. The tradition of floating gardens is one which still survives today, as melons and tomatoes are mostly grown on them. Akbar paid three separate visits to the valley and liked to refer to it as his private garden. When there, after a six-weeks journey, he would relax, go water-fowling and beating and watch the saffron fields being harvested in the autumn, accompanied by his son Salim, whose love for Kashmir would be even more obsessive than his father's. These Kashmiri pilgrimages are celebrated, for successive emperors had gardens made at stopping places along the way. It is a measure of the peace and security which Akbar had established in northern India that he could absent himself in such an inaccessible spot.

The centre of Kashmir is Srinagar, and it was to the heart of this lush valley with its saffron fields on Lake Dal that successive emperors went, building around the lake their superlative gardens, no less than seven hundred in the time of Jahangir. However, Akbar's first building was the fortress of Hari Parbat, which dominated the lake, and later the garden palace of Nasim Bagh.

Following the Timurid tradition, Akbar had started to build his own tomb at Sikandra near Agra before his death, a building which his son finished. It is a monolithic structure in red sandstone with marble inlay, sitting four-square in a quartered garden, proportioned to set off the great tomb. The scale foreshadows later Mughal building, as does its predecessor, Humayun's tomb in Delhi; but the interconnecting water channels to the tanks are still narrow, although they are now contained in a stronger axial plan. The garden today lacks the classic planting of cypress, pine and plane and the life which running water would have given it. It is however a fine tribute to perhaps the greatest of the great Mughals.

JAHANGIR (1569–1627)

Akbar, a master stateman, had stabilized the Mughal dynasty and so prepared the way for Jahangir. He came to the throne at the age of thirty-six, having accompanied his father willingly or unwillingly during many journeys and been party to the making of many great decisions. In

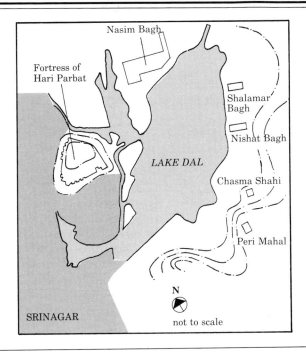

Map showing Lake Dal with labels: Nasim Bagh, Fortress of Hari Parbat, Shalamar Bagh, Nishat Bagh, LAKE DAL, Chasma Shahi, Peri Mahal, SRINAGAR, N, not to scale

character, however, Jahangir was more like his grandfather Babur, whom he followed in keeping a regular diary and whose gardens he visited in Kabul. We know much of Jahangir's life from these diaries; compared to previous emperors, his life-style was comparatively quiet, his only real troubles coming from within his own family.

Jahangir, one suspects, was not particularly interested in statesmanship, his talents being directed more towards the arts. He was guided in the first and helped in the second throughout his life by his wife, Nur Jahan.

We know that, if Jahangir did not illustrate his diaries himself, he had artists to do it for him and they showed a keen interest in natural history. We know too from the diaries of Sir Thomas Roe, ambassador of James I who spent four years in India, that Jahangir exhibited strong interest in European portraiture and that this influenced the Mughal school of painting. These interests, combined with a love of the landscape of Kashmir (inherited from his father, along with his passion for building), produced in Jahangir a garden designer of no mean talent and, indeed, the central proponent of Mughal garden art. Jahangir in turn was followed by his son Khurram, later to become Shah Jahan, and together they built the finest Kashmiri garden, the Shalamar Bagh. Nur Jahan shared this design interest with Jahangir although she also displayed interest in palace

ABOVE *Map showing the location of surviving Mughal gardens round Lake Dal at Srinagar in Kashmir.*

interiors and golden ornamentation – when she was not exhibiting her political acumen. Together they visited Kashmir many times, spending whole summers there, and the gardens, some of which Jahangir started when still a prince, were progressively improved and enlarged by them. The royal gardens of Shalamar, Achabal and Verinag belong to this period, together with Nur Jahan's own garden on Lake Manashal, known as Jarogha Bagh. Her brother Asaf Khan also developed the largest and most spectacular of them all at Nishat Bagh. In his diaries, Jahangir describes the minutiae of the gardens, with details of the flowers growing there and the general feasting and jollities of their summer days there. Again, following the family tradition, Jahangir suffered from alcoholism and a dependence on opium; these gardens make an ideal background in which he could have indulged himself, surrounded by the rich and opulent court life lived outside. Jahangir also suffered from asthma and the Kashmiri height would have alleviated this.

At this time the court and capital moved with the emperor. Delhi had not been raised to the standard it reached under Shah Jahan, and Jahangir visited it only as often as he went to Ajmer, Lahore or Agra. Perhaps it was because it was further north than Delhi and therefore nearer to Kashmir that Jahangir made Lahore his real capital. Near it Nur Jahan laid out the huge garden of Dilkusha at Shahdara; here Jahangir was eventually buried in a tomb of his wife's design, while Nur Jahan and her brother were buried close by.

A stopping place on entering Kashmir, and one of the many caravanserai along the way at the foot of the Banihal Pass, was an ancient place of worship called Verinag. Though less spectacular than some of the more famed of Jahangir's gardens surrounding Lake Dal at Srinagar, this layout has a direct and uncomplicated simplicity that is very moving. A spring emerges in a deep clear pool stocked with mammoth carp – their ancestors are reputed to have had golden rings inserted in their noses by Jahangir. The pool is encapsulated in a colonnaded building, one side of which was a bridging palace over the water channel which runs out of it. The stone-edged channel runs between two huge chenars straight as a die for nearly three hundred metres before dropping into a stream reputed to be the source of the Jhelum river. Behind the domed roof of the colonnaded building, the last outpost of the mountains rises sheer upwards, clothed in dense greenery. This bold and simple use of a canal of water is a foretaste

OPPOSITE LEFT *Plan of the gardens (laid out in 1609) at Verinag in Kashmir, situated some 75 km south-east of Srinagar. Water rises in a carp-filled octagonal pool and flows in a wide canal through surrounding gardens down to a stream.*

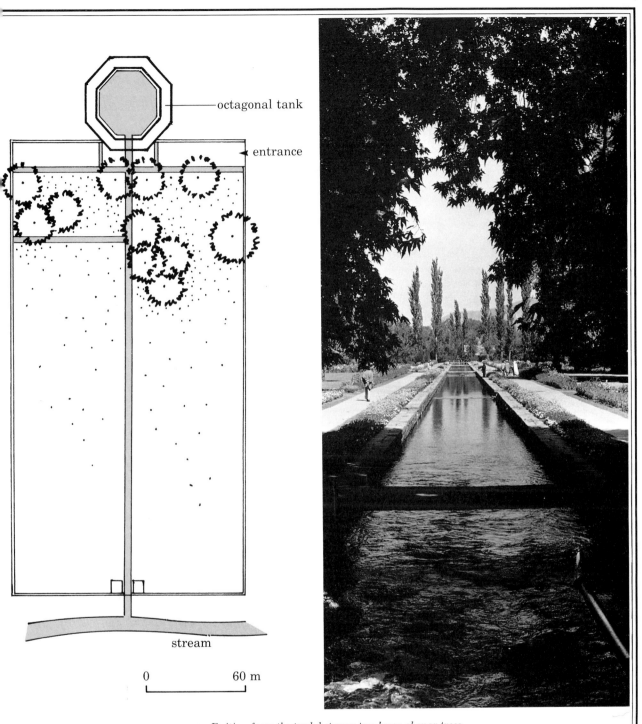

octagonal tank

entrance

stream

0   60 m

ABOVE RIGHT *Exiting from the tank between two large chenar trees,*
the stone-edged canal at Verinag runs straight for 300 m
to its stream outlet. Summer flowers line the canal.

139

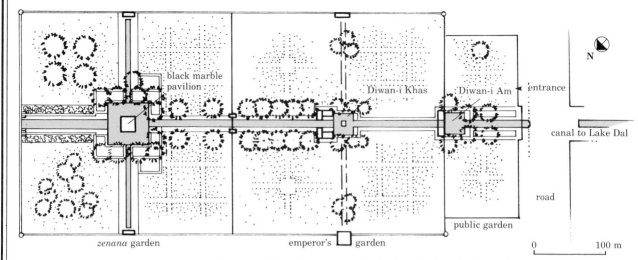

black marble
pavilion

Diwan-i Khas

Diwan-i Am

entrance

N

canal to Lake Dal

road

public garden

zenana garden

emperor's garden

0   100 m

ABOVE *Plan of the Shalamar Bagh, Kashmir (built in 1619), showing
the progression of pavilions and outside 'rooms' to the top of the garden,
beyond which rise the mountains that feed the gardens with water.*

of joys to come as subsequent emperors progressed through the terraced rice fields, fruit and walnut orchards of Kashmir to their lake at Srinagar. Lake Dal had always held a fascination for the Mughal emperors, and visions of carved wooden houseboats basking among floating islands of greenery and fields of pink lotus and yellow water lilies were not an illusion. The water is crystal clear and deep, mirroring the background of sharp mountains as they rise up from it, to end against a jagged horizon, sprinkled with straggling conifers.

Across the lake from Srinagar lies the most famous of Jahangir's gardens – the Shalamar Bagh. It should be approached across the water at leisure, for this is how the emperors visited their gardens. Now a road runs round the lake and actually crosses this garden and its near neighbour, Nishat Bagh. On plan these gardens have an affinity with those of Renaissance Italy but in actuality there is none, for, particularly at Shalamar, the progression or build-up is from the lowest part up to the highest, whereas in Italy the reverse is more often true. So the experience of a Mughal garden or palace is similar to that of entering a mosque: one of progression. The rhythm of the progression, however, lies in water; in this sense there is a similarity with Italian gardens, but its use is different: seldom for baroque display, more for calm, being always cool and restful. The pedestrian in the garden is almost incidental and his path accompanies the water and weaves round or over the waterfalls and watercourses in it. The water linking the levels sometimes cascades in great unbroken sheets, or rushes headlong down stone ramps, called *chadar*, whose surface is broken to increase the rippled effect.

The true *raison d'être* of these gardens is as a place for contemplation and sitting cross-legged on carpets by the waterside, or on stone or marble benches straddling the stream for coolness, the sound of adjacent falls of water and fountain jets muffling conversation; or, as at Shalamar, as a place for the emperor to sit in his Hall of Public Audience, the Diwan-i Am, its gaily painted ceiling above the black marble throne lit by reflections from the surrounding pool. The courtly aspect of these gardens is carried through in their function, for the linear progression up the garden is from the Hall of Public Audience to the Hall of Private Audience, to the living and women's quarters, the *zenana*, to which only the emperor himself had access. Each building is surrounded by its own garden area. At Shalamar this progression is also followed so that the famed black

OPPOSITE BELOW *A low stone bench sits astride one of the numerous cascades of the Shalamar Bagh, providing a cool secluded spot for conversation or contemplation amid the splendour of the surrounding mountains.*

The black marble pavilion at Shalamar has a later Kashmiri wooden roof,
but the black marble columns still remain. Recesses behind the cascade
(reminiscent of those in the miniature on p. 121) would have held
colourful cut dahlia heads by day and candles by night.

marble pavilion of the *zenana*, built by Shah Jahan, is the culmination of
the garden layout and is ringed about with delicate plumes of water, an
exercise in quiet delicacy and meticulous detail, a casket for the jewels.
Behind the last pavilion the mountains rise up, and in front there is a
quiet descending order of harmonies in pavilion and water within an
avenue of massive chenars, until at the end of the canal sits the tranquil
lake.

While one is aware, when considering earlier Islamic gardens, of the lack
of domestic building as a focal point in the layout, only in Kashmir is the

true ideal achieved, the ideal of paradise described quite explicitly in the Quran as a series of pavilions within a garden, an ideal predating that of Timurid tents within their enclosure, the whole concept in fact being of a 'palace without a roof'. Some essence of such a format was present in the disposition of the buildings at Fathpur Sikri as well. The complexity of the Alhambra's interpenetration of garden with building masks this ideal, although the basic format is there, because the palace pavilions have become concentrated in such a limited site. Tombs, which the Western mind would regard as replacement dwellings, are in fact pavilions in a landscape, and this central structure is invariably accompanied by boundary structures acting as stops to the accompanying water channels.

A Persian quotation appears at Shalamar which reads: 'If there be a Paradise on the face of the earth, it is here, it is here, it is here.' Its layout would indeed seem most nearly to aspire to the Quranic ideal. The garden was built both by Jahangir and by Shah Jahan as a young man, the father using his flair for site and location, the son his exquisite taste for building. It is far less showy than nearby Nishat Bagh and less worldly than Achabal but justifies its reputation as one of the world's most beautiful gardens.

Nishat Bagh, a little way along Lake Dal from Shalamar, was not built as a royal garden and there are fewer pavilions within its layout, since ceremonial was obviously less frequent. It is reputed to have been made by Jahangir's brother-in-law, Asaf Khan, Nur Jahan's elder brother. The siting of the garden is far more spectacular than at Shalamar, being tucked more into the mountain, and it has a far steeper ascent, so contains larger features as well. Water flows faster and cascades are greater but, while a magnificent concept, it somehow loses the tranquillity of Shalamar. The garden has been further improved by the recent removal of a pavilion across the centre of the site which, though originally allowing a view through its watercourse, was latterly blocked.

Like its neighbour, Nishat Bagh should be approached by water from the lake through a bridge in the *bund*, or old made-up road through the lake. From the inner pool beyond the bridge the *bagh* reaches out to embrace the visitor with arms of chenar planted right down to the water's edge. From this point there ascends a progression of differing levels to the ultimate *zenana* terrace and central pavilion which bridges the water's entrance into the garden. Originally there were twelve levels, one for each sign of the zodiac, but this number has been reduced owing to the road

The view down to Lake Dal at Nishat Bagh, Kashmir, which was supposedly built by the brother-in-law of Jahangir in 1625. A floating causeway planted with trees and pierced by a bridge provides a watery forecourt for boats approaching across the lake.

bisecting them. The garden is now approached from the lake between two pepper-pot pavilions, with a cascade between them, the wall containing the cascade being festooned with brilliant blue morning glories. Feeding this great cascade, now tumbling down to the roadside, is a wide canal running the length of the garden and punctuated at regular intervals by spouting fountains. At each change of level there is another cascade or a rushing, rippling *chadar*. The flow is fast and the garden wide and open, so that the mood is altogether more lively than at Shalamar. The ultimate, private *zenana* terrace is retained by an arched wall six metres high and flanked at either end by balconied pavilions reminiscent of medieval gazebos and allowing a similar view for the women, once lodged in them, to the outside world.

A water chute at Nishat Bagh connecting the top
zenana *gardens to the next level.*

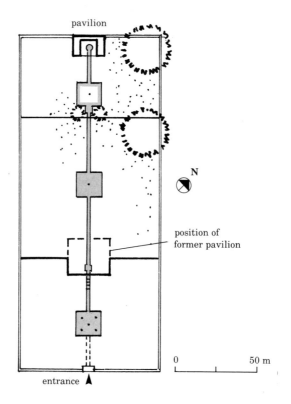

pavilion

position of
former pavilion

N

entrance

0   50 m

While the changes of level are so dramatically stated by water features
and catchment pools and reinforced by flanking flights of steps, there is
strangely no linking paving between them, following the stone edging of
the canals. The direct access path up the garden is to one side of the canal
complex. The whole *zenana* terrace is grassed over and planted with huge
chenar and clumps of fruit trees. The view from this ultimate terrace is
spectacular, down the garden and across the lake to the hill beside old
Srinagar on which Akbar's fort, the Hari Parbat, is superbly sited. A
feature of Nishat is the placing of stone or marble thrones across the
watercourses, which make a perfect complement to the canals – to sit upon
them with water rushing beneath is a delight. It is so near to Shalamar,
which is composed of similar features in a similar setting, yet so very
different.

Still on this mountainside of Lake Dal there is another smaller garden
than Nishat Bagh or Shalamar known as Chasma Shahi, or the Royal
Spring, for it was built around the course of a renowned water source. The

ABOVE *Plan of the small Chasma Shahi garden in Kashmir
built in 1632 and attributed to Shah Jahan. Water flows across
three descending levels and originally went through
a central pavilion, though this has now been removed.*

garden was built in 1632 and is attributed to Shah Jahan. The garden has been altered over the years considerably but its strong axial layout is interesting, though the concept is now somewhat negated by the recent removal of the central pavilion which was built in the Kashmiri style. Originally, the spring emerged, bubbling up through a marble lotus basin in an existing pavilion at the top of the garden, the private *zenana* garden, from which it still flows to a regular tank with a single jet. From here the water flowed into the now removed pavilion to appear and fall immediately down a steep *chadar*, narrow like a slide, to end in another fountained pool which stands at the centre of the lowest little garden. This axis is visually continued through a stone gateway and on. Without its pavilion, which must have had a ravishing view along the lakeside below, this garden is lost, and the subsidiary pavilion containing the watercourse, tucked into this mountain surround, has gained a primary significance for which it was not intended.

The other major extant garden in Kashmir is some way from Lake Dal,

ABOVE *The view from the pavilion at the top of the garden of Chasma Shahi,*
which is situated on a hillside above Lake Dal.
Until recently a pavilion stood at the end of this vista
and must have commanded a panoramic view over Lake Dal.

but on the old direct route to it from the south via Jammu. It is Achabal and, like Verinag quite close, it is set into the mountains. Supposedly the work of Nur Jahan, Jahangir's wife (the *begum*, or queen), it was originally called Begumabad for that reason. Smaller than both Shalamar and Nishat Bagh, it combines some of the qualities of both, being lively with strong rushing waters, as at Nishat, but nevertheless achieving a feeling of serenity as at Shalamar. It seemed a country version of the more urbane lake gardens. The build-up of the garden as in a palace is again from bottom

Plan of the garden at Achabal, situated about 50 km south of Srinagar and set into the mountains at the source of a sacred spring. Water descends into a large tank and through two pavilions before entering a channel which leads into a river at the bottom of the garden. It was supposedly built by Nur Jahan, Jahangir's wife.

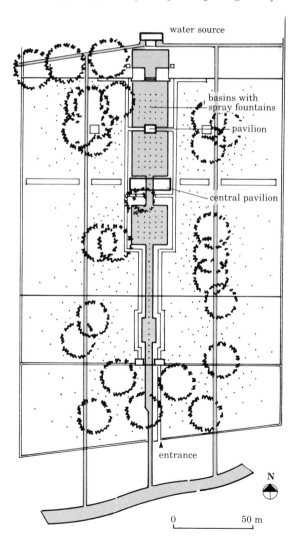

*Like a stream of pure light the main watercourse at Achabal
runs through the deep shade of huge chenar trees.*

to top as one progresses through it. Sadly, original Mughal buildings have been replaced by Kashmiri ones, the smaller of them lacking architectural subtlety; but their disposition nevertheless remains very much in the 'palace without a roof' tradition. The watercourse flowing through and round the buildings is superb, dappled by the shade of massive chenars. The ultimate fortissimo of the garden is a massive waterfall seemingly pouring out of the mountain, but in fact collected from a famous sacred spring which is renowned for the sweetness of its waters and a place of pilgrimage for centuries. The plan of Achabal is strong and simple and perhaps unique in that two side channels parallel the main one as they all tumble down the terraced levels of the site. The infill planting of fruit trees has now gone and simple broad stretches of grass replace them.

Interestingly, Shah Abbas of Persia and Jahangir were contemporaries, and the artistic achievements of their respective countries were at their

highest during their lives, with the place of the garden being high on the list. Both were Muslim, their courts were opulent, receptions were grand and drink flowed freely. Gardens and pavilions provided a background for this rich life, as interwoven and entwined as the pattern which often adorned them. But the building materials, the occupants and the locations – sometimes friendly, sometimes hostile – were very different. The gardens and pavilions reflect this difference.

SHAH JAHAN (1592–1666)

Although Shah Jahan had been involved with his father, Jahangir, in the layout of the Shalamar Bagh and did visit Kashmir more than once again, his own territory was much more the plains of India owing, no doubt, to his being more Rajput than Mughal through both his mother and his grandmother. Jahan's great genius was for building and planning, though the gardens in which the edifices sat were no less important than those of his father in Kashmir. However, being erected on flat ground and encompassing a structure, they returned to the Persian *chahar bagh* tradition, although they were now much enlarged and the narrow water channels became smooth canals. Under his patronage, painters specialized in lifelike representations of birds, animals and flowers.

Shah Jahan's first masterpiece, the Taj Mahal, was built to the memory of his legendary wife Mumtaz Mahal, whose death, only three years after Jahan came to the throne, affected him deeply. She died while giving birth to her fourteenth child; of the previous thirteen children, four sons and three daughters had survived. The eldest son, Dara Shikuh, was born in 1615 and the third, Aurangzeb, in 1618, and round these two the inevitable Mughal struggles for succession centred during the second half of Shah Jahan's life. His life underwent a change from one of continual campaigning in the field to a more sedentary one, controlling his sons, to whom he delegated military responsibility, from his courts at Agra, Delhi or Lahore.

Jahan concentrated now on his building and planning projects. The first was the Taj Mahal. Shah Jahan had been interested in architecture from

OPPOSITE *Water cascades down from the water source at Achabal to flow under the first pavilion, which is set across the centre of a large tank.*

ABOVE *An unusual view of the Taj Mahal, Agra, seen across the garden
which was largely planted during the Taj's restoration by
Lord Curzon in 1903. Built by Shah Jahan as a tomb for his legendary wife
Mumtaz Mahal, the Taj was completed in 1654.*

an early age, and while various names are accredited to the design of the
Taj, it is thought in the end that Jahan used the proposals which he
commissioned to crystallize his own thoughts on the design of this personal
mausolem to his wife. The building was begun in 1632 and was the logical
conclusion to several strands which already existed in Mughal building.
The swelling shape of the dome above the pointed *ivan* is a design concept

OPPOSITE *The main watercourse leading up to the Taj Mahal is interrupted
by a raised tank from which secondary water arms, now dry, run into
the surrounding garden. The tomb is not central to the garden,
possibly because Shah Jahan had intended to build his own tomb in black marble
on the other side of the river Jumna, which runs behind the white
marble building of the Taj. The river would have then been the main
cross axis. Note the star of Islam decoration bordering the main watercourse.*

straight from Persia. The slender flanking minarets had a predecessor in the gateway to Akbar's tomb, and the white marble inlay had been used in another tomb, that of Itimad al-Daulah at Agra, built by Nur Jahan for her parents. But most of all, the Taj Mahal was a development of the tomb form, seen perhaps in embryo in the tomb of Humayun built in 1564, but reaching full Mughal flower in this exquisite building which was completed in 1654.

The garden form, too, had progressed from that of the early squared layout, brought from Kabul by Babur, and first seen in India at the Ram Bagh; for from it the layout surrounding Humayun's tomb in Delhi had developed, to gain in importance and have a more strongly linear feel, and from this in turn grew the reflecting canal which mirrors the Taj Mahal so famously. Some essence of Jahangir's layouts in Kashmir, and his broad use of moving channels of water, must also have become infused as well. The building is smaller than one anticipates, and the white marble of which it is made brings it to life in a way in which the dead red sandstone of tombs does not, for the marble reflects the sun and moon quite differently at all hours of the day and night.

The main building of the Taj Mahal is flanked by sandstone and marble pavilions, one a mosque, the other a reception hall, while the main tomb sits on a plinth between them and above the level of the quartered garden. There is a raised marble platform at the junction of the long canal with its lesser, and now dry, side arms. The building itself is so enthralling that few people go into the surrounding lush garden, now planted in park-like fashion. The whole complex is surrounded by a crenellated wall, restored in 1903 by Lord Curzon.

The Taj building, which one approaches along the length of its reflecting watercourse, is so unlike all the other tomb buildings because it is not central to its site; beyond it there is a sharp drop down into the Jumna river. It was said that Shah Jahan had intended to build another mausoleum in black marble for himself to face his wife's across the river, although this project was never realized. An intriguing theory is that, had the other tomb been built, joined by a bridge across the river, the two tombs would have been combined to form a central pavilion complex, divided by surely the largest canal ever. Half a kilometre to the left of the Taj, up a broad sweep in the river, is the low profile of the Red Fort, encapsulating Shah Jahan's pearly marble quarters in which he spent his last sad years.

OPPOSITE *Plan of the Anguri Bagh, which was built by Shah Jahan within the* zenana, *or women's quarters, in the Red Fort at Agra. The Khas Mahal, where Shah Jahan would have sat, overlooks this quartered garden, the four sections of which would have been planted with brightly coloured flowers creating a remarkable carpet effect.*

In 1638 Jahan moved his capital from Agra to Delhi, though not before he had altered the Red Fort at Agra, pulling down Akbar's buildings along the top of the wall and replacing them with his own characteristic white marble palaces. Throughout the building of these, Jahan was also able to oversee the work at the Taj. In Delhi, Shah Jahan founded a new city called Shahjahanabad, which is now known as old Delhi to distinguish it from Sir Edwin Lutyens' New Delhi. Between this and the river, Jahan built a new fort, surrounded by a red sandsone wall similar to that of the fort at Agra.

The entrance to the fort in Agra through the massive red wall is impressive and, despite the beauty of his personal buildings within it, Shah Jahan must have felt very much a captive there in later years. The inner courtyards with their trees have the enclosed and restful quality of the Tower of London or a university quadrangle; through the courtyards one progresses to the Anguri Bagh, or *zenana* (women's quarter), and the

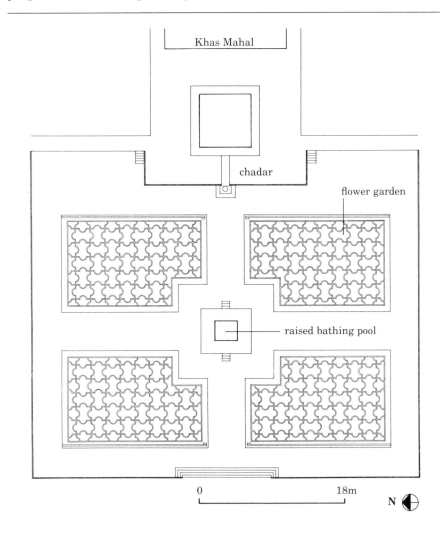

Khas Mahal

chadar

flower garden

raised bathing pool

0   18m

N

From the Khas Mahal Shah Jahan could have watched his ladies bathe in a central marble pool (foreground), surrounded by flowers on all sides.

private paradise/palace, the Khas Mahal. This quartered garden with a raised marble central tank is a traditional Mughal parterre. At one time it must have blazed with colour; now it is rather bare and blinding white in the sun, though intended to be seen from the cloistered balconies above rather than from ground level. The central tank was obviously a bath, linking to another larger one in front of the Khas Mahal sitting on its plinth. The larger pool has a fluted marble edging. Visually the two are linked by a marble cascade, similar to those of Kashmir in that they contain niches in which were placed flowers by day and lights by night, to be seen through the falling water. There is a deserted sadness about this garden when one remembers that in happier times Shah Jahan celebrated the marriage feast of his two sons, Dara Shikuh and Sultan Shuja, here. The whole of the marble complex of the Agra Fort has a deserted feel about it, calling for water in its empty basins and the rustle of silk and music. It has the aura of a stage set without a performance.

In another courtyard, the Machchi Bhawan or 'Fish Square', the area also lies barren, robbed of its fountains and basins by the Jats of Bharatput in the eighteenth century. These gardens are disappointing, although the intimate scale of Shah Jahan's marble pavilions adjoining them is marvellous and their workmanship and interweaving layout exquisite. These regal domestic buildings are paralleled by the Taj, which gleams across a reach of the Jumna. The internal shallow marble pools, their inlay, the magnificent lace-like feeling of worked marble screens, the views open and closed, above and below, are all breathtaking. They seem a refinement on even the Alhambra's rooms, and are equally evocative.

Shah Jahan connected Agra, Delhi and Lahore by an avenue 640 kilometres long, bordered on either side by trees. Again at Lahore he made his contribution to the fort originally made by Akbar. Niccolao Manucci – an Italian gunner and part-time doctor in the service of Jahan's eldest son, Dara – wrote of these Mughal palace forts, saying that they were

full of gardens with running water, which flows in channels into reservoirs of stone, jasper and marble. In all the rooms and halls of these palaces there are ordinarily fountains or reservoirs of the same stone of proportionate size. In the gardens of these palaces there are always flowers according to the season. There are no large fruit trees of any sort, in order not to hinder the delight of the open view. In these palaces are seats and private rooms, some of which are in the midst of the running water. In the water are many fish for delight.

Prince Dara Shikuh, having proved himself incompetent in the struggle against his brother (he was later killed by Aurangzeb), retired to mystical study which had always interested him. Whatever his other deficiencies at family intrigue, Dara Shikuh must have inherited his father's eye for splendour, and his grandfather's love of nature, as his choice for a site – above Lake Dal – on which to build a school of astrology for his tutor, Akhund Mullah Shah, was inspired. High up the mountainside behind Chasma Shahi is Peri Mahal, the 'Fairies' Palace', and it lived up to its magical name in its siting. Originally a rather grandiose layout, with a central building and flanking pavilions, it sits upon a podium with, behind, stepped terraces rising to a central pavilion.

The site has recently been cleared and a precipitous road laid up to it. Traces of fountains and tanks can be seen in the newly planted garden, though the interconnecting waterways must have been underground since there is no trace of cascades or *chadars* between them. This is one of the loveliest sites in all Kashmir.

After killing another brother, Murad, Aurangzeb proclaimed himself emperor in 1658. For the next eight years Jahan was held impotent in a state of open imprisonment within his beautiful marble palace inside the Agra fort, looking towards the mausoleum of his wife, while Aurangzeb, the son he liked least, slowly annihilated the rest of his family, including Prince Dara Shikuh.

Shah Jahan died in 1666, the most glittering of the great Mughals and the one who brought the great tide of Mughal building to its climax, achieving a perfect fusion with the surrounding landscape. He was buried beside his wife in the Taj Mahal.

AURANGZEB (1618–1707)

Although on the death of Aurangzeb the Mughal empire was little more than halfway through its history, it could be said that he was the last of the great Mughals. Manucci, an old man now, claimed that Aurangzeb left seventeen sons, grandsons and great-grandsons who could wrangle and murder over the future succession, so weakening the empire that it fell easy prey to a later attack from Persia.

Aurangzeb himself was something of a religious zealot, and bigotry, once allowed its head, is difficult to restrain. Many restrictions were practised against Hindus and other minorities under the veil of Muslim righteousness, paralleling to a degree that of the Christian Inquisition in once Muslim Spain. It was this confrontation of Muslim and Hindu which led to the partition of India and the foundation of East and West Pakistan and its mass communal massacres more than two and a half centuries later. However, Aurangzeb practised privately what he preached publicly: for instance music was prohibited at court, as were effeminate styles of dress; alcohol was forbidden and the cultivation of cannabis made illegal. The documentation of any history of the reign was also forbidden, pre-

OPPOSITE *The spectacular site of Peri Mahal, the 'Fairies' Palace', built by Dara Shikuh, Shah Jahan's son, as a school of astrology high above Lake Dal in Kashmir. Several levels of the garden have recently been restored but it still lacks its original water tanks and fountains.*

sumably for reasons of modesty. Thus, in one stroke the emperor had condemned many of the vices and – it must be said – much of the pleasure of the Mughal court. Such pleasure had been visual as well as sensual and had fed expression in both garden and building. However, to his credit, it must be said that Aurangzeb did build some superb mosques: the Pearl Mosque within the Red Fort at Delhi continued the fine marble tradition of his father, Shah Jahan. In literature Aurangzeb had little interest other than in sacred works or the repertoire of classical Persian verses. Surprisingly, painting fared better, although little was done to maintain the imperial studio, with the result that artists drifted away to minor courts to continue the Mughal tradition there.

The early part of Aurangzeb's reign was given over to suppressing the remainder of his family. Later in his life he moved south, relinquishing the stability of the sumptuous court life of Delhi or Agra and embracing the sterile and nomadic one of continual campaigns in the Deccan. Here, Aurangzeb's arch-enemy was the chieftain of a small guerilla band called Shivaji, who, by successfully avoiding confrontation with Aurangzeb while continually harassing him, was to become a twentieth-century symbol of Hindu endurance against Muslim oppression.

Aurangzeb's long reign is of interest for the light it throws on his predecessors' achievements. It was thanks to travellers such as Bernier, Tavernier and Manucci that details of gardens remain. Bernier especially left the most complete descriptions of the gardens of Kashmir.

Aurangzeb died at the great age of eighty-eight in 1707, while still campaigning, his life at the end having become not dissimilar to that of his nomadic Mongol ancestors. As a contrast to the impressive tombs which had been a feature of previous Mughal rules, Aurangzeb's own tomb at Khuldabad near his southern capital of Aurangabad in the Deccan is extremely modest. Throughout his life he spent any time which he could spare from state affairs making copies of the Quran by hand. These were sold, and he directed that only money from these sales was to be used on the construction of his tomb, which is a small square enclosure with a plain marble wall surround.

Aurangzeb's rule was in fact one of comparative poverty, the exchequer having been depleted by Shah Jahan's magnificent building programme. Aurangzeb's tomb to his first wife at Aurangabad is a rather weak copy based on the design of the Taj Mahal. The splendour and sure-handedness

OPPOSITE *Aurangzeb's tomb for his first wife at Aurangabad, which was based on the design of the Taj Mahal. The superfluity of elements, constructed largely in plaster, tends to create an unrestful effect at odds with the whole point of a tomb building.*

of the Taj is replaced by a confusion of superficial elements, constructed (for economic reasons) largely in plaster and clearly showing that the climax in design had been passed.

Of the next eight great Mughal emperors whose combined reigns spanned no more than fifty-two years, four were murdered, one deposed and only three died peacefully on the throne. The strength of the great court ebbed and the princely states of India took on an identity of their own again which they retained under the subsequent British 'protection'. The Mughal emperors themselves becoming virtual puppets in the hands of differing factions. Parallel with the decline of the Mughals in India was that of the Safavids in Persia, who after the Afghan sack were displaced by Nadir Shah, a Turk from Khurasan, in 1736. Two years later, Nadir Shah invaded India and, in a triumph only equalled by Timur's Indian invasion, entered Delhi, sacked it and returned to Persia with a thousand elephants, a hundred masons and two hundred carpenters, together with jewels – the Kuh-i Nur and the Peacock Throne amongst them. The throne was later broken up and rebuilt under the Qajar Fath Ali Shah.

The complex relationship of cultural strands between Persia and Mughal India was now broken, and the golden thread running through the relationship had always been Islam. Interestingly enough, currently the new Iran is aligning itself on a political level with Muslim Pakistan, the seeds of whose origins were sown during Aurangzeb's futile campaign against the Hindu Deccan.

NORTH AFRICA, EGYPT, SICILY AND THE OTTOMAN EMPIRE

NORTH AFRICA

So far we have bypassed any influence which might have originated from the southern seaboard of the Mediterranean since few gardens of any size now remain. However, during its long and chequered development within Islam, important influences did spread from this region first to Sicily, which in turn influenced Italy, and later and more importantly to al-Andalus. What does remain to be seen on the African mainland has in its turn been influenced by Spain, concluding a cycle.

Settled life in North Africa was possible only within a narrow coastal strip, and most of the main centres of trade and culture were to be found within this area. Throughout their history these centres were subject to constant attack from the sea, a situation not conducive to garden-making. However, trade flourished and the coastal cities, while looking east to Egypt and into the heart of Islam, west to Spain and north to the Mediterranean, were also at the head of the trade routes which stretched across the Sahara desert to the south. Goods were exchanged and also ideas, which were disseminated as far afield as Samarkand and China. So the ebb and flow of Islamic thought continued to wash these shores, contrasting with the ideology of its own indigenous population,which on the one hand was settled and Arabic, and on the other was Berber and nomadic. The history of North Africa is therefore complicated.

When the Arabs first arrived in the middle of the seventh century they brought no particular architectural style; but since North Africa formed a part of the Mediterranean world which the Arabs knew of already in Syria, the style which evolved was ostensibly the same in both areas. The Syrian prototype had perhaps a greater Persian influence, particularly in decoration, while in North Africa greater simplicity prevailed; but their underlying unity was clear. Syrian influence was later reinforced via al-Andalus while, at the same time, eastern developments infiltrated from Egypt and later from Ottoman Turkey.

The Aghlabids governed a part of North Africa including Ifriqiyya (roughly modern Tunisia and eastern Algeria) and Algiers from AD 800 to 900. They were important as builders of cities, palaces and pleasances, and as the first Muslim conquerors of Sicily in AD 827; however, they could not withstand the incursions of the Fatimids.

Until the appearance in North Africa of the Fatimid dynasty in AD 909, the history of Islam in North Africa was chequered, with no particular group unifying the whole area, although the khalifal suzerainty of Baghdad was generally acknowledged. However, their supremacy did not last long and challenges from rival clans reduced the area under their control to Egypt alone.

Between 1050 and 1052 the Fatimids launched two Arabian tribes into North Africa from Egypt, who devastated the area and caused the complete ruination of settled agriculture. While these invasions were taking place, the first of the two great Berber empires was formed in the far west, which affected the course of Andalusian history. First the Almoravids (1056–1147), originating south of Morocco, launched a wave of conquest and eventually crossed to Spain in 1086. They could not, however, withstand the second Berber wave, the Almohads, but by then the Almoravids had conquered southern Spain, bringing Andalusian culture into direct contact with North Africa for the first time and causing the life of North African cities to become imbued with the customs and traditions of urban Spanish society. The Almohad empire (1130–1269) was also fairly short-lived, becoming vitiated through family in-fighting and the formation of rival dynasties.

The Almoravids left little by way of architecture in Marrakesh, their main centre, but the great mosque in Algiers is essentially a Berber structure as is that of Tlemcen (Algeria), which is basically unaltered and

·contains certain features similar to those of the great mosque in Cordoba. The strong Spanish influence can be seen in most monuments.

The Almohads continued the theme of their predecessors, but pared much its extravagance. The most notable remains are the three great minarets, those of Kutubiyya in Marrakesh, the Hasan tower in Rabat and the Giralda in Seville, now the belfry of the cathedral.

By the middle of the thirteenth century, North Africa was again divided under feuding Berber dynasties; however, of importance during this time was the influence of Andalusian refugees, fleeing first from the advance of the Christians into al-Andalus and later from the rigours of the Inquisition. Hand in hand with this influence went another, that of the rise of holy men – marabouts – in North Africa, and a subsequent proliferation of tombs and *zamiyas* where Sufi brotherhoods would meet. Orthodox madrasas and mosques were also built, and their architecture was strongly influenced by the Andalusians; city life also benefited from these urban Spanish Muslims.

ABOVE *A small paved patio in the Bardo Palace, Algiers, with a central water tank and a typical arcade of horseshoe arches.*

The Marinids (1196–1549), who ruled Morocco after the Almohads, continued their Spanish tradition and built Fez as their new capital. With their rival neighbours, the Zayyanids (1235–1554), who ruled mainly from Tlemcen, and the Hafsids (1228–1574), who ruled Tunisia and eastern Algeria after the eclipse of the Almohads, these Berber dynasties ruled North Africa until the sixteenth century when the whole area was acquired by the corsairs for the Ottoman empire. This succession was now at an end, and the North African world turned in on itself.

What can be deduced of the garden tradition during this time was that there were broadly two types of enclosure. The first, known as a *riyyad*, was the typical small, paved, urban patio, flanked on two or more sides by galleries or covered ways. The garden was quartered by marble, tiled or brick paths with a small pavilion or fountain in the centre. The areas of planting were sunk below the level of the intersecting paths to facilitate the watering of orange trees, and included an underplanting of flowers, possibly roses, for scent. Such was the typical Moroccan town garden,

ABOVE *A walled terraced garden in Rabat, Morocco. Cultivated areas are sunk below the formal layout of paths to facilitate irrigation, and vegetables as well as flowers are planted beneath larger fruit trees.*

which was clearly based on Persian precedent though subsequently over-laid by Andalusian influence and expertise in irrigational techniques.

There was also a second, larger country garden tradition known as the *arsa* or *agdal*, which often took the form of terrace gardens, designed in typical squares for easy irrigation. These gardens were for pleasure, though fruit was sold from their orchards. Oranges, lemons, pomegranates, apricots, bananas, quinces, figs, apples, plums and pears were grown against a backdrop of cypress, mulberry and olive. Vegetables as well as flowers were planted beneath the trees to supply the royal households which the gardens primarily served.

Further external inspiration, being of Andalusian culture rather than created locally, was reflected in an architecture of refined and detailed decoration, which eventually became repetitive and fussy, while the structures themselves lacked originality. This introspective attitude continued until the revitalization of the coastal towns by Turkish influence in the sixteenth century.

ABOVE *The Agdal gardens outside Marrakesh, Morocco, with the Atlas mountains in the distance. A vast tank provides irrigation and was once also used for pleasure boats. Originally laid out by the Almohads in the twelfth century, these extensive gardens with their rows of olive trees probably attained their present form in the mid-nineteenth century.*

Semi-independent Turkish dynasties were created in Algiers, Tunis and Tripoli under the general suzerainty of the Ottoman sultans, and these states continued to flourish until the eighteenth century, affecting garden concepts little, though the more ornate painted kiosks and balustrading of wrought iron might have been a Turkish introduction. The fusion of Turkish and North African culture did, however, produce an architecture that was new. It was also the great age of Tunisian tilework. Most of the tile panels which decorated the mosque of Tripoli, and the fountains of palaces and castles, originated in Tunisian workshops. There was also a continuing indigenous vernacular architecture, that of the courtyard-house style, which is still apparent in Algiers and Tripoli, as well as in Morocco, epitomizing that affinity with enclosed space and inward-looking life-styles that is typical of followers of Islam everywhere.

EGYPT

In contrast to the areas so far considered Egypt is unique in having retained a geographic integrity throughout its history – the present borders being virtually the same as those at the first unification of the country in the fourth century BC. This stability encouraged a continuity of habit in Egypt despite changes in people, religion or politics – indeed the agricultural methods used up to the nineteenth century were almost identical to those of earliest times. The prodigality of Egyptian agriculture was made possible by two factors: firstly, the river Nile and its inundation, assisted by a complex system of canals and basins, and secondly, a growing season lasting the whole year and enhanced by the possibility of growing plants from both temperate and tropical regions. Subsequently vegetation in the Nile Valley did not have the rarity value so important elsewhere in the Middle East.

Almost all the plants depicted in the abundant wall paintings and models of Ancient Egyptian gardens, the waterlilies and papyrus in the pool, the surrounding date palms, persea, pomegranate, fig and jubejube trees, and the arcades of vines, produced an edible or useful product. Although the species utilized increased greatly, this horticultural practicality was to remain the keynote throughout Egyptian history. Royal palaces and temples incorporated much more elaborate gardens: Hatshepsut's 'Gardens of Punt', Tuthmosis III's exotic Botanical Garden and Akhenaten's Menagerie are just three well-known examples. Other 'healing' temples were surrounded by plantations of medicinal herbs. During Greek, Roman and Byzantine times (third century BC to seventh century AD) these practices continued, but the latter part of the period saw the triumph of Christianity and the rise of monasticism. To defend themselves against predatory tribes the monks surrounded their complexes with massive walls inside which they had wells watering large gardens and orchards.

The Arabs in general, while retaining ancient agricultural practices, rejected the Christian cultural traditions, and the major early influences were from the khalifal metropolis first at Damascus and after AD 763 Baghdad. Little is known of the lives of the earliest Muslim inhabitants who after the conquest of Egypt by Amr ibn al-As in AD 640–42 built a new capital, Fustat (the present Old City of Cairo), on the site of a Roman fortress.

For 200 years Egypt was governed as a province of the khalifate, but in 868 one of the governors, Ahmad ibn Tulun, was powerful enough to claim independence, in celebration of which he founded a new city, al-Qatai, just north of Fustat. He established a dynasty lasting until 905 from the latter years of which we have archaelogical evidence of houses and accompanying gardens. Externally the houses formed irregular alleys which belied their regular interiors where several rooms faced a small paved courtyard in which a *salsabil* (conduit), served by a sophisticated water system, led to a fountain and pool surrounded by shrubs and plants.

In 935 the Abbasid khalifate regained control of Egypt and installed a client dynasty, the Ikhshidids, as rulers. The last capable ruler, the Sudani eunuch Kafur, had a vast garden laid out by the side of the main canal. Literary sources describe its many kiosks and pavilions.

After the death of Kafur in 968, the Fatimids, a Shiah dynasty who had been established in Tunisia for about sixty years, invaded Egypt in 969. Of Syrian origin, they had assimilated much of the North African cultural tradition and introduced many artistic innovations into Egypt. Their political ambitions were very different from those of their predecessors. Totally opposed to the Sunni Abbasids, they made claims to the

میان غرب وجنوب باغ حوض که در دسی است اطراف تمام

درختهای نارنج است درختهای انار هم هست گرد اکر دحوض تمام

سه برکه زار است جای عین باغ همینت در وقت زردشدن

انارهای بسیار خوب می انها میخیلی باغ خوبی طرح شده و طرف

*Like the illustration on p. 127 this Mughal miniature from another version
of the Baburnama of c. 1590 shows the Bagh-i Vafa near Kabul in 1508.
Despite the differences between these two representations of the same garden,
some basic features such as the abundance of water, the quartering of
the garden by canals and the fruit trees (the pomegranates and
orange trees described in Babur's memoirs) remain constant in both pictures.*

ABOVE *Mughal miniature of c.1565 showing a mythical figure, Rustam, with his mistress in a garden pavilion.*

OPPOSITE ABOVE *Akbar's tomb at Sikandra near Agra, India, built between 1604 and 1613, sits at the centre of a quartered garden. Originally cypress, pine and plane trees would have scaled down the immensity of the building.*

OPPOSITE BELOW *The black marble pavilion at Shalamar Bagh in Kashmir is surrounded on all sides by water and fountains.*

ABOVE *At the Achabal gardens in Kashmir water passes under*
a pavilion (just visible in the background behind the trees)
and into a pool with fountains (in the foreground) before descending
through the rest of the gardens to a river below.

OPPOSITE *A cascade crashes over the lower terrace*
at Shalamar Bagh in Kashmir.

TOP *The ruins of the gardens of Peri Mahal, Kashmir,*
set high up in the mountains above Lake Dal.

ABOVE *A garden in Marrakesh, Morocco, with a formal quartered layout.*
The citrus trees in the surrounding beds are sunk below the level
of the pool, facilitating irrigation.

OPPOSITE *The spectacular Nishat Bagh, Kashmir. Its descending garden 'rooms'*
are dissected by a water channel with a rippling chadar *between each level.*

The Courtyard of the House of the Coptic Patriarch, Cairo, *1864,*
by J. F. Lewis. The architectural style of the house belongs to
the Mamluk period (1250–1517) and the well-shaded courtyard with
a column and pool has a talar-*like appearance. The painting*
is an example of the 'orientalist' school of the period
and captures the mood of the middle eastern domestic scene
typically located in an outside 'room'.

spiritual leadership and styled themselves khalifs. They built a new walled capital north of Fustat naming it al-Qahirah, of which the focal point was al-Azhar Mosque. Two immense palaces were built either side of the main street, the Eastern Palace for the administration and the Western Palace, which incorporated the Garden of Kafur, as the home of the royal family. In this garden among the myrtles and pomegranates the child al-Hakim (reigned 996–1021) had his guardian Barjawan assassinated and began his terrifying career as khalif. Only a few buildings remain from the Fatimid city but their love of nature is apparent in their arts, the carved wood and stucco, metalwork, fabrics and ceramics are decorated with a riot of arabesque foliage through which myriad animals caper and birds fly.

Although by the eleventh century their boundaries were reduced to Egypt alone, the Fatimids continued with their massive propaganda programme, the effects of which are apparent today in their spiritual descendants the Ismailis and related Shiah sects. Salah al-Din, a Sunni who was among the Zangid armies sent to assist the Fatimids against the crusaders, seized his opportunity and in 1169 the Fatimid khalifate was quietly eliminated. He consolidated his control on Egypt and enclosed the whole Fustat/al-Qahirah complex within massive walls, siting his Citadel in the south-eastern corner. His subsequent campaigns and the establishment of the Ayyubid dynasty are well known. Vast areas of Fustat had been burned in an attempt to forestall occupation by Crusader forces and these were cultivated as a park, described by the French traveller Thenaud in the fourteenth century as 'a sumptuous and large garden full of all kinds of fruit trees ... irrigated by water from the Nile'.

The last effective Ayyubid sultan, Nagm al-Din (1240–49), built up a vast slave army (mamluks) of Crimean Qipchaq Turks who through an extraordinary turn of events established themselves as rulers. The Mamluk dynasty was to last nearly 300 years (1250–1517), controlling also Syria and the Hijaz. At almost the same time the seat of the Abbasids' khalifate was transferred from Baghdad to Cairo and, although merely a figurehead, the khalif enhanced the prestige of the sultan. All the powerful sultans were products of the complex slave systems, the main source changing later to the Caucasus, but despite the internal power struggles of the amirs (nobles) a remarkable cultural succession was established, giving rise to a unique Egyptian style.

Preferring horse pasturage and sports fields to gardens the Mamluks nonetheless appreciated beauty and were great patrons of the arts. In the Citadel the palace was rebuilt on a magnificent scale and contained a menagerie and gardens. Perhaps the Mamluks' attitude to horticulture can be summed up by two examples. The consuming interest of one of the most powerful of the sultans, al-Nasir Muhammad (1294–1340), was sheep and he kept a flock of several hundred in the palace grounds – the effects on the vegetation can be imagined. On another occasion gardens were taxed at 100 dirhams per acre, the same rate as prime agricultural land; it provided little incentive to grow flowers.

The Old World traveller, Ibn Battutah (1304–78), mentions all the cities he visited during his travels and in describing Egypt quotes an earlier poet, Nahid: 'The bank of Cairo is a garden unparalleled'. Throughout his journal of Egypt, Syria and Iraq his references are always to gardens in the sense of informal orchards – a view confirmed by other literary sources – and thus this would seem to be the preferred type of garden in the central lands of medieval Islam.

Sultan al-Ghawri (reigned 1501–16) had a large portion of the parade ground below the Citadel dug up and planted as a garden, which he stocked with imported pheasants and deer. Here he would sit in a vast tent and present each amir with a rose. He was the Mamluk sultan whose forces were defeated by Sultan Selim in 1517, after which Egypt declined to the status of an Ottoman province.

Along with the khalif, most of the Egyptian craftsmen were taken by Selim to Istanbul, as a result of which Egyptian culture suffered greatly. Mamluk decorative features were retained but imposed upon Ottoman building, two new types of which are particularly important in the garden context. The first were the domed mosques built by some early governors in the metropolitan style of Constantinople. As in Turkey they were surrounded by a garden enclosure watered by conduits and fountains. Several of these mosques still stand in Cairo although sadly the gardens have disappeared: the Mosques of Sulayman Pasha (1528) and Sinan Pasha (1571), and the Mosque of al-Malika Safiyya (1610) that the Venetian wife of Murad III wrested from her chief eunuch. Among her provisions for the mosque she included 'two men understanding plants, trees, herbs and their improvement and irrigation' and 'two strong men charged with watering the plants'.

The second innovation were *takiyyas*, hostels for sufis of various brother-

hoods. Here cells surrounded an arcaded courtyard, in the centre of which a raised garden contained a fountain with channels leading to an ablution tank. Two of these are still extant in Cairo with their gardens: the Takiyya of Sultan Sulayman II (1543) and the Takiyya of Sultan Mahmud II (1750). Similar Ottoman foundations exist in Syria and Iraq and it seems that this was the closest these areas were ever to come to creating the 'little paradise'.

Throughout the Ottoman period the Mamluks had gradually regained their ascendancy but only briefly managed to make Egypt independent prior to the French Occupation (1798–1801). From Napoleon came the first systematic description of Cairo since the Ottoman conquest, during which period domestic architecture had changed very little. Napoleon's first headquarters was in the Palace of Qasim Bey, in his description of which he writes, 'The garden was filled with fine trees but there was not a single path. A large trellis covered with vines and heavy with grapes proved a welcome find.' In the *Description de l'Egypte*, the magnificent

ABOVE *An 1839 engraving of the courtyard of the Takiyya (sufi hostel) of Sultan Sulayman II in Cairo, which was built in 1543. Cells open onto a cloister surrounding the garden, which contains a kiosk and fountain.*

179

product of the Institut de l'Egypte which he set up in Cairo, there are several illustrations of palaces, the interior courtyards of which are filled with date palms, bananas and smaller shrubs.

Muhammad Ali came to Egypt from Macedonia in 1801 among the Ottoman forces raised to expel the French. In the resulting debacle and by manipulation and deception he rose to be the supreme leader. Acknowledged by the Ottoman sultan in 1805, he founded a dynasty that was to last until 1952. With him the old cultural traditions were abandoned, victims to his passion for European technology and methods. Among his many European advisers he employed several gardeners who laid out the gardens of his palaces. His favourite was the Shubra Palace, where the gardens were a showpiece, visited by many European travellers. Winding paths led among beautiful shrubs to the Fountain Kiosk (now a casino), where loggias surrounded a huge white marble pool and an island fountain.

Ibrahim (died 1848), son and successor to Muhammad Ali as well as being a great military commander, had a passion for trees, which he planted profusely to beautify Cairo, his English gardeners completely transforming Rawdah Island. He was succeeded by the xenophobe Abbas I, who, although he reversed many of his predecessors' policies and dismissed the advisers, did retain a Scottish gardener, Mr McAdam. The

OPPOSITE ABOVE *An engraving from the* Description de L'Egypte *(published in 1809) of an interior courtyard of the Palace of Qasim Bey, Cairo, with wide* talars *and lush tropical foliage.*

BELOW *Another engraving from the* Description de L'Egypte *depicts the gardens of the Palace of Qasim Bey. The palace was Napoleon's headquarters during the French occupation from 1798 to 1801, and he describes a vine-covered trellis which can perhaps be seen on the left of the picture. The random planting of the garden shows more affinity with European traditions than anything Islamic.*

BELOW *An engraving of the garden of the Shubra Palace,*
Cairo, built by Muhammad Ali, showing the loggias surrounding
the huge pool and island fountain.

profligate Khedive (1863–79) Ismail during a visit to Paris admired the landscaping of Barillet-Deschamps and invited him to Cairo, where he set out the Azbakiyya Gardens, centrepiece of Ismail's restoration of the city, and the gardens of the palaces on the Gazirah and at Giza. The latter can still be seen as the Urman Gardens and the Zoo. Pebbled mosaic paths lead through raised beds, and in the centre is a strange 'petrified forest' now inhabited by baboons.

The major achievement of his son Tawfiq (1879–90) was the Muntazah Palace at Alexandria. A vast park surrounded the palace, a copy of the Palazzo Vecchio in Florence. Strange follies are interspersed with stands of foreign palms, underplanted with bushes and flowerbeds, where formerly herds of gazelle were free to wander.

By the twentieth century the taste for the exotic had triumphed: gardens were either landscaped in the European manner or given over completely to fantasy – perhaps the most extraordinary of these being the Indian Temple of Baron Edouard Empain at Heliopolis and the Japanese Gardens at Helwan.

SICILY

There can be no doubt that gardens flourished in Sicily when it was ruled from Algeria by the Aghlabids after their partial conquest of it after AD 827. At this time it was under the Abbasid khalifate. But the whole island did not come under Muslim rule until as late as 962, when Palermo finally fell. However, the form the gardens took is vague, as the subsequent Norman conquest in 1091 completely destroyed them. The crusader Roger Haulteville and his descendants so identified themselves with local life in Sicily that they became known as the Christian sultans. Yet, from contemporary descriptions and the remains of their buildings, it would seem that their gardens and way of life differed little from their Muslim predecessors.

An Arab poet who visited Palermo during the reign of the last Norman in the second half of the twelfth century said that 'the King's palaces and gardens were disposed around the town of Palermo like a necklace which ornaments the throat of a young girl.' From the evidence which we have, garden courtyards did exist, very much along the lines of those in North Africa and presumably not dissimilar to those in Cordoba too, but the land surrounding the buildings was designed more as a pleasure park, part of which was the garden, modelled on the lines of the Persian *paradisos*, but most of which was for hunting. The fact that these gardens disappeared early would indicate that their layout had little influence on later Renaissance gardens, although their fame would have kept alive the tradition of the pleasure park. We also know that the early Muslim invaders brought the citrus from North Africa and that it was later introduced into the Renaissance garden of Italy, the scent of orange and lemon blossom being one of its great charms.

There is an orchard garden laid out in grid form at the palace of the Mare Dolce in Palermo, which would suggest that it may have been modelled on an Arab original. Evidence of Arab influence, too, is obvious in the water *chadar* (seen in both Spanish and Mughal gardens) at the palace of the Ziza, also in Palermo.

The carved marble chadar *at the Palace of Ziza in Palermo, Sicily, which clearly reflects Moorish and Mughal traditions.*

OTTOMAN EMPIRE

We know very little of the layout of early Turkish gardens, although their beauty is remarked upon in writings from quite early times. Comment is always, however, on content rather than pattern, and an inherent love of flowers and colour would lead one to suppose that the idea of the quartered garden found no foothold here. This was not the case, although the formation was by now traditional rather than functional, since the coastal Turkish climate makes irrigation unnecessary. But early formal gardens under the Ottomans must have been as common in Constantinople (Istanbul), as in Kabul, Herat, Agra or Granada, and Isfahan was nearer than any of them; its development under the Safavids was contemporary with early Ottoman power.

It might be supposed that the horticulture of the Ottoman sultans after 1453 would have owed a great deal to the practice of their Byzantine predecessors, and thus ultimately to classical Greece and Rome. But this is not so, for the tulip, so distinctive a feature of both Turkish and Persian art, is not depicted in any Byzantine work of Constantinople. So both the character of Turkish gardens, and the plants in them, indicate a derivation from the east, probably from Persia and the common Islamic garden tradition, which was crystallized by the Turkish dynasties who ruled from Bukhara and Samarkand. This was the tradition, as we have seen, which Babur carried into India.

Large building complexes in Turkey had always tended to be defensive, and it was not until 1326 that a new type of open planning was conceived in the building of the city of Bursa by the Ottomans, in which their buildings were sited at random in the landscape. This was a totally new conception, and one made possible only by the builders' complete assurance of their supremacy.

Christian Constantinople fell to the Ottomans in 1453, the capital being transferred there from Bursa. This Byzantine city, which had been tightly contained within city walls, now started to expand outwards and along the Bosphorus. The harem of the sultan, Mehmed II, was sited on a promontory above the Bosphorus and, like other royal enclosures within Islam, developed as a series of pavilions with different functions within a garden setting. This was Topkapi, which had a population of 25,000.

We know that Mehmed, after the completion of his own palace, ordered his chief courtiers to build themselves grand houses too. His commander-in-chief, Mahmud, built a mosque, a food kitchen for the poor, inns and baths, and also 'planted gardens with trees bearing all sorts of fruit for the delectation and happiness and use of many, and gave them abundant supply of water.' Finally, about 1455, we are told by Kritovoulos in his contemporary account of Mehmed the Conqueror that the pleasure grounds around Topkapi were complete: 'Around the palace were constructed very large and lovely gardens abounding in various sorts of plants and trees, producing beautiful fruit. And there were abundant supplies of water flowing everywhere, cold and clear and drinkable, and conspicuous and beautiful groves and meadows.'

This random layout of Topkapi is obvious today, and while many of its individual buildings contain courtyards and pools in strong Islamic tradition – which is not surprising, given the Turkish tradition of formalized pattern and function – no broad theme holds them together. It was really only the mosque in Turkey which took on a distinctive architectural form, typified by the Ahmediye (Blue Mosque) complex, built between 1609 and 1612.

During the reign of Suleyman the Magnificent (1520–66), 'gardens were gay with hyacinths, narcissus, tulips and roses. The sad cypress trees kept watch over the humble tombs. Suleyman enjoyed walking amid delicate

The Revan Kiosk (built in 1635) with its pool and fountain is one of many kiosks and pavilions in the Topkapi complex, Istanbul.

gardens and graceful fountains where he would sit under the shade of a plane tree and compose a poem. Suleyman's chief gardener held sway over the whole government of the seraglio, and the sultan's palaces on the shores of the Bosphoros and the Sea of Marmara. It was his duty also to arrange the royal hunts, steer the sultan's barge, and preside over the execution of great men. Twenty-five hundred gardeners were under him . . . .'

Evliya Celebi, whose story of his Asian and European wanderings earned him great renown, dwelt at length on the gardens which he saw on his travels. His account of the Turkish gardens of Istanbul and Edirne in 1631 is very interesting. According to him, every royal garden was encircled by either cypress or pine trees. In the middle were flower beds in geometric designs where roses, hyacinths, violets, tulips, jasmine, jonquils, narcissi, lilies, stocks, peonies, carnations and sweet basil bloomed, each set in its private triangle or square. He also mentions the beautiful honeysuckle- and jasmine-covered kiosks, the terraced fountains and the bright garden paths of shells and coloured pebbles winding their labyrinthine way

ABOVE *A Turkish miniature of 1734 showing palaces and other buildings with gardens along the Bosphorus.*

OPPOSITE ABOVE *A sixteenth-century representation of a court in Topkapi, Istanbul. The garden appears to be planted in a random way with cypress and plane trees, and to be stocked with deer – rather in the manner of a paradise park.*

OPPOSITE BELOW *A court in Topkapi with the Ahmediye, or Blue Mosque, in the background.*

through the courtyards and gardens. Sultan Murad IV (1612–40) is quoted as saying, 'Even I do not possess such a garden of Eden!', when he visited a courtier's garden on the Bosphorus. He took delight in sitting in the shade of a horse chestnut tree, 'its candles just starting alight in the April air, watching a fountain that dripped in the ivied wall. A thread of water started mysteriously out of a marble niche falling into a little marble basin, from which it overflowed by two bronze spouts into two smaller basins below. From them the water dripped back into a single basin still lower down, and so trickled its brooked way, past graceful arabesques and reliefs of fruit and flowers, into a crescent-shaped pool at the foot of the niche. Every sort and size of tree was there, but the greatest number of them were of a kind to be sparsely trimmed in April with a delicate green, and among them were so many twisted Judas trees as to tinge whole patches of the slope with their deep rose bloom.' These layouts sound more European than Islamic!

It was the travels of Pierre Belon in the Levant in 1546–8, and his writing on botanical species which he found there, which focused the increasing horticultural interest of the Western world upon Turkey, and so started the first major wave of exotic plants westward from it. Another pioneer, noted by John H. Harvey in his *Turkey as a Source of Garden Plants*, was the imperial ambassador Ogier Ghiselin de Busbecq, who was in Turkey between 1554 and 1562. He and members of his entourage, and later merchants encouraged by the success of his mission, were responsible for the sudden flood of species which reached Vienna, Antwerp, Paris and London. The plants sent from Turkey were almost entirely varieties already in cultivation there. They were not, as with most subsequent introductions, found in the wild, but had already been improved by centuries of culture, grafting or accidental hybridization. And most of these, apart from a few species that had found their way from China with the caravans on the silk route, were the result of Muslim gardening over a long period.

By a process of deduction, based on the species known to have been introduced into Europe before 1600 from Turkey, one can work out which plants must have existed in the gardens of Constantinople and the other royal cities of the Ottomans: Adrianople, Bursa, Manisa, and Smyrna. Quite early, the West had received the oriental plane tree, the black mulberry and, indirectly, the walnut, hollyhock, white jasmine, scarlet

OPPOSITE *A sixteenth-century Turkish painting of a flower festival at the court of Sultan Murad III. The tulip was already becoming the focus of wide horticultural interest, which was to reach its climax during the Lale Devri or 'Tulip Period' of the early eighteenth century.*

campion, peony and opium poppy. These were followed by the horse chestnut, certain crocuses, Byzantine gladiolus, day lily, purple primrose and the sweet sultan. But it was through Turkey that the great bulbs arrived: the crown imperial, hyacinth, *Lilium candidum*, muscari, anemones, various narcissi and the tulip.

The Turks shared an adoration of the tulip with the Persians and later it was to become a cult plant in Europe. During the reign of Ahmad III,

(1703–30), which became known as the Lale Devri or 'Tulip Period', Turkey became the floricultural centre of the world, and tulip bulbs became so expensive that many varieties were re-imported from Holland. They were valued above all other flowers and became the symbol of pleasure and elegance: tortoises with lighted candles on their backs were set loose amongst the tulip beds during night festivities. The sultan's tulip fields in summer pastures above Manisa are legendary and, as John H. Harvey points out, the fact that the great botanist William Sherard was British Consul at Smyrna, only forty kilometres from Manisa, from 1703 to 1717, may explain the recording of these royal city gardens.

The tulip was not only adored in gardens for its colour; it was also used as an ornament or decoration in mosques and on fountains and tombstones, appearing too as illustrations in manuscripts and books, and also on tiles. Tahsin Oz, in his book *Turkish Ceramics*, states: 'In the tiled buildings of Istanbul, which were built in the sixteenth century, 276 types of tulip have been distinguished. Some Western scholars ascribe this wealth of floral ornament in Turkish tiles to the great love of Turks for flowers, and in illustration of this they point to the fact of the importation of 500,000 hyacinth bulbs for the Sultan's palace in 1579. And travellers relate, that from Edirne onwards to Istanbul, they have seen endless fields of hyacinths, tulips, narcissi. In mosques hyacinths, sweet basil, violets were scattered along with rose water.'

The other great love shared by Turks and Persians alike was the rose. For the Turks, roses were not merely flowers to look at and smell, ablaze even in the smallest garden: they ate them, drank them and bathed in them. A Turkish host would have offered a bowl of rosewater for bathing the face and hands, and possibly a long, cool drink prepared from rose petals. In the evening, liqueurs prepared from the essence of roses might be drunk, but the supreme achievement was rose-petal jam.

The significance attached to the constituent parts of the garden, combined with an increasing European influence (the Ottomans' rule extended into central Europe as late at 1922 when the sultanate was abolished), resulted, not surprisingly, in a diffusion of the clarity of the traditional Islamic garden with European elements. The whole became divided into separate areas of horticultural interest. The baroque, too, crept into its form and detailing, to provide a curious mixture of styles still to be seen in the sumptuous villa gardens along the Bosphorus.

WATER AND PLANTS IN THE ISLAMIC LANDSCAPE

Two further themes – water and plants – need to be considered and amplified in this survey of the history and development of Islamic gardens. The fundamental importance of water in the structure and form of gardens has already been discussed, but its use and significance extends further in both functional terms, affecting traditional social organizations, and in artistic terms, as a decorative feature. Water can be seen as the connecting link between the historic gardens of Islam and their modern successors in Arabia, and will continue to be so in any garden or landscape throughout the region. It is not only a physical necessity but also has great religious significance. Not surprisingly, rules and rituals have sprung up in the usage of so valued a commodity, here exemplified by the *falaj* system of the Gulf States.

TRADITIONAL WATER SYSTEMS

The underground water system in Iran is known as the *qanat*, in North Africa as the *fujrah* and in the Gulf as the *falaj* – although *qanats* are sometimes built as part of the *falaj* – and round this system a settled way of life has evolved. It is estimated that 90 per cent of the rainfall in Oman enters aquifers (rocks or deposits containing water), so little is wasted,

and they are tapped by wells or *falajs*. Broadly, the word *falaj* means a system for the distribution of water among those who have established rights to a source of supply, and the word is used to encompass the whole of the irrigation channel system downstream of where the water originates. Thus it may describe a water channel which has tapped a flow in the upper gravel of a wadi, or stream bed, and been constructed alongside it, to lead the water away for distribution; or it may be carved into rock walls of a wadi for several miles. It may also mean a man-made water mine in which water has been stored in an aquifer and is then brought to the surface by means of a tunnelled conduit or *qanat*.

ABOVE LEFT *A typical* falaj, *or water channel, in Oman traces a snake-like route through a palm grove.*

ABOVE RIGHT *A precipitously situated* falaj *brings water to terraced fields in Oman.*

At the root of village life is the need to preserve water rights, and the distribution of water is therefore carefully controlled and recorded in *falaj* books. In a single *falaj* there may be as many as two hundred owners of permanent water rights, alongside owners of temporary rights as well. A reasonably sized *falaj* of the *qanat* type may support more than a thousand people and produce a flow of about nine gallons per second to irrigate an area of some forty hectares of permanently cultivated land. Nearly all of this perennial water from the *falaj* is used for the date palms, although citrus, bananas, pomegranates and mangoes may well also be watered. Outside the palm groves lucerne (alfalfa) is planted in characteristic squared earth basins, and grain or leguminous crops are then grown from the surplus water discharged from them.

A strict system of priorities is also in force for human needs when the water first comes to the surface. Drinking has first priority, and all have free access. In a residential area there is then a descending order of priorities: bathing, a vital function in Islam, comes first, with the men's bath upstream of the women's and each contained in its own little enclosure; then the place where the dead are washed. Mosques may have direct access for their own ritual ablutions. Only after these basic human demands are satisfied are there specific offshoots from the main stream for land use. Ensuring the continuance of these priorities, along with the maintenance and cleaning of the channels, is the responsibility of the communal *falaj* organization, while individuals are responsible for the channels in their own gardens. Thus, a man draws his private water supply from a fixed point for a fixed period, and for this he pays.

Much agricultural work is carried out on a communal basis as well: the watering of the palms, the cutting of the dates, the fertilizing of the female flowers and the tying up of the date bunches. This work, for which he is paid in kind, is carried out by the *bidar*, who is responsible to the *arif*, or supervisor of the water channels, not to the owners of the palms. The *bidar* does no weeding – this is done by the *haris*. These traditional farming methods have been practised since pre-Islamic times, and the whole closely knit system with regional variations is in use throughout the settled areas of the Gulf.

The fabric of settled village life is then based on a knife edge, a juggling of amenities available to combat the overwhelming and often extreme elements of the climate for, as one moves south from the traditional centres of Islamic culture, life becomes even harder. Any deviation from the established pattern may cause chaos and death through starvation; for example, if too many trees are taken for fuel, the source of food and fodder is affected, and there is less shelter and shade, and therefore a lack of recycled elemental nutrients to encourage the growth of other food supplies beneath the trees. The resultant bare soils encourage erosion, and an excess of blown sand results in irreversible loss of vegetation and fertility. In the East man is still tied to his landscape, as a part of it, in a way that largely disappeared from the Western world centuries ago.

The rigours of this life-style, combined, until recently, with a mainly nomadic population (away from the settled coastal strip), accounts for the lack of development in traditional garden forms in Arabia, although in such a climate the internal courtyard form of domestic building takes on an even greater significance. The scarcity of water and the multiple uses to which it was necessarily put allowed little extra for extravagant display, even if it could be afforded.

WATER AS A DECORATIVE FEATURE

In more sophisticated surroundings the usage of the water becomes quite stylized: water channels become decorative, and the holding tank becomes a pool for reflection in secular use and a brimming cistern for ritual washing in the mosque. Where water sources are plentiful, as in mountainous Kashmir, the water channels are not only decorative but display the inventiveness of their creators too; when sited on the flat lands south of Kashmir, the reflective pools become enlarged to a canal. Thus the different ways in which water is shaped and moulded depend on its use. Within these channels of varying widths, of differing depths and speed of movement, the water is used in different ways as it traverses its site, for to obtain movement change of level is obligatory.

The Mughals exploited this change-of-level idea to its fullest extent, although similar, if smaller, features appear throughout Islam: for instance, the cascade crashes over the levels of Achabal and the Shalamar garden at Lahore; the *chadar*, seen in Spain and in Persia, becomes a mighty chute at the Nishat Bagh; and at a later garden at Udaipur, that of the Sahelion-ki-Dair, the use of falling water from the roof of a circular pavilion creates a watery curtain to surround it.

Change of level allowed for the earliest development of the fountain, at first no doubt a cascading spout of water, and only later developing with the use of pressure into the free-standing fountain which is so dominant a feature of the Islamic garden. The pressure in early fountains was created by building up a reservoir of water above their location, then leading the water from it in pipes of ever-decreasing diameter so that, with the downward weight of water in a diminishing aperture, the thrust is

A mighty water chute at Nishat Bagh, Kashmir, connects
one level of the garden to the next.

increased, until the water gushed out at the fountain head. It was then distributed in a single plume, and only later through a rose nozzle to be sprayed or sprinkled in a variety of ways, to cool the air and create different patterns of cooling sounds. We know that the original Mughal fountain heads were shaped like lotus buds and were made of brass. The earliest known Islamic fountains are to be found in Spain; again the recurrent motif there is that of the lotus, which is used in both fountain and bowl. The lotus motif must have been imported, since the plant does not grow in Spain.

The most famous early fountain is that in the Court of the Lions in the Alhambra, although it is now generally agreed that the carved lions themselves probably date from the eleventh century while the basin set over them was not made for that position and is of fourteenth-century construction. The author of *The Alhambra*, Oleg Grabar, has put forward the interesting thesis that the lengthy inscription by Ibn Zamrak which surrounds this basin contains two important themes. One is that of the fountain as the prince who encourages and rewards his soldiers, the lions of holy war. The monument itself, a water basin supported by animals, is a common enough type with many known parallels, but in the context of the Alhambra it is provided with the specific meaning of royal victory within a royal pavilion and, as so often in Islamic art, it is not the forms themselves which express this meaning, but the writing inscribed on them.

ABOVE *Water falls in a curtain from the roof of a late Mughal pavilion in the garden of the Sahelion-Ki-Dair at Udaipur.*

The other theme the inscription contains is that water can be seen as a solid substance, like a sculpture or monument, or at least as giving the illusion of sculpture; water, in other words, becomes a work of art. It is this latter theme which the Mughal gardeners took up and exploited so brilliantly to cool their open-air palaces, visually as well as physically.

The tradition of larger sheets of water is of fairly recent date but, where it is employed first on quite a small scale (as at Fathpur Sikri, later in Lahore and then in the Zand and Qajar gardens in Shiraz), it is always part of a formal layout, fitting into an overall plan and fed by a continuous natural stream. This tradition does not translate well to the climate of the Gulf States or Saudi Arabia, where continuous water is an expensive and precious commodity, quickly evaporating in the sun. This practical hazard has not deterred its current usage on the grand scale, however, and, what is worse, its use in the manner of the eighteenth-century English landscape school within contoured land forms. Such a conception, though no doubt

A superb lotus water basin in the Rang Mahal building at the Red Fort at Delhi. Originally decorated with an inlay of semi-precious stones, the basin is carved from marble and the central fountain is shaped as a floating lotus bud.

manageable – at a cost – would seem to ignore the 1,400-year-old traditions and Quranic aspirations of the paradise garden. Within the parameters of these precedents, it should still be possible to use water in a traditional manner, though updated by modern methods of containing and conducting it.

Interestingly, a major advance in the use of water has been the adaptation of the brimming ablution tank into the brimming swimming pool; the usage has become secular, but the function is not dissimilar. The blue-tiled interior of the swimming pool has a direct precedent in the blue-tiled pools of Persian tanks of water, as seen at the Bagh-i-Fin. In the West, the private swimming pool is still something of a status symbol; in the

ABOVE *The central fountain of the Court of the Lions at the Alhambra.
The carved stone lions date from the twelfth century, although
the fountain basin is probably fourteenth century. One of the themes of
the inscription surrounding the basin likens water to a solid substance
like a sculpture, implying that water itself can become a work of art.*

198

developing hot lands of the Middle East it is more of a necessity. Furthermore, it is in use the whole year round and often becomes a major part of the layout, for it inevitably becomes a social focal point as well. In this way it again recalls parties of Timurids, grouped on carpets by the water's edge, with the former pavilions being used for more mundane functions such as changing clothes or filtering water.

PLANTS

Attitudes to plants and planting in the Middle East are equivocal. On the one hand there is a great love of flowers, and their colours and scents, as well as the need for, and appreciation of, the shade of fruit trees, as outlined in the Quran; on the other, there is little concern for natural vegetation, where there is any, nor any great botanical interest in either indigenous or introduced species on the domestic scale. Again, tradition and the climate are at the root of this ambivalent attitude. Islamic literature does not manifest a great love of wild nature – rather it advises a walled retreat from it – perhaps because there are few areas of wild flora and fauna which would evoke a Wordsworthian love of nature. Combine this with the fact that subtropical agriculture is a great source of disease – cholera, hookworm, bilharzia, dysentry and typhoid all spread via irrigation channels – and one soon realizes that one is not likely to return refreshed and renewed from a day in the country!

For many people, the concept of garden, whether public or private, is comparatively new. However, stories of the beauties of various flowers are legend, based on the paradise concept. We have seen the use of plants constantly in symbolism within Islam, and early Andalusian poets made much of the rose and the nightingale. Later, Persian poetry abounds with horticultural allusions, particularly to the rose. Chardin, visiting Persia in the seventeenth century, said of gardens there:

There are all kinds of flowers in Persia that one finds in France and Europe. Fewer kinds grow in the hotter southern parts but by the brightness of colouring the Persian flowers are generally more beautiful than those of Europe. Along the Caspian coast there are whole forests of orange trees, single and double jasmine, all European flowers, and other species besides. At the eastern end of the coast, the entire land is covered with flowers. On the western side of the plateau are found tulips, anemones, ranunculi of the finest red, and imperial crowns. Around Isfahan jonquils increase by themselves and there are flowers blooming all winter long. In season there are seven or eight different sorts of narcissus, the lily of the valley, the lily, violets of all hues, pinks, and Spanish jasmine of a beauty and perfume surpassing anything found in Europe. There are beautiful marsh mallows, and, at Isfahan, charming short-stemmed tulips. During the winter there are white and blue hyacinths, lilies of the valley, dainty tulips and myrrh. In spring yellow and red stock and amber seed of all colours, and a most beautiful and unusual flower, called the clove pink, each plant bearing some thirty blooms. The rose is found in five colours, white, red, yellow, Spanish rose, and poppy red. Also there are 'two-faced' roses which are red on one side and yellow on the other. Certain rose bushes bear yellow, yellow-white, and yellow-red roses on the same plant.

From personal observation, many, many others of our common European garden flowers could be added to this list, growing both wild and under cultivation.

This great Persian love of flowers was translated into the making of artificial flowers and trees, and we know that in the Ghaznavid period the court was enhanced with trees of gold flanked by artificial narcissi in pots. At the later Timurid courts in the thirteenth and fourteenth century, similar trees are featured, of which the most elaborate appear to have been for Timur himself, in his royal tent at Samarkand. This man-made tree, the height of a man, bore leaves like those of the oak, while its fruits were of pearls, rubies, emeralds, sapphires and turquoises. Little birds of coloured enamel perched upon the branches. This same love of flowers led to their being depicted on the carpet, often as a background infill to the layout of a *chahar bagh* – a tradition which moved, with that of miniature flower paintings, into Mughal India. Mughal emperors were enormously interested in and appreciative of Kashmiri vegetation, and we have quite detailed accounts of the planting of some of their gardens and orchards. The authors of *The Gardens of Mughal India* have listed the species portrayed in their miniature paintings – in Kashmir and Lahore: the carnation, delphinium, hollyhock, jasmine, lilac, lotus, narcissus, saffron, stocks and wallflowers; in the region around Delhi and Agra: carnation, coxcomb, heliotrope, hyacinth, jasmine, larkspur, love-lies-bleeding, lotus, marigold, narcissus, oleander, tuberose, violet and zinnia – to which might

OPPOSITE *Persian miniatures glow with the artists' love of plants and flowers. In this Persian miniature of 1430 a prince and princess meet in a garden bursting with plants, which include flowering almonds and pomegranates.*

be added from what European records existed cyclamen, iris, tulips, crown imperials, lilies, pinks, roses, poppies and peonies.

So there is in Arabia a very strong traditional appreciation of plants. But the climate there has in the main denied the inhabitants both a settled existence in which to cultivate, and little enough water where they did so to irrigate crops and fruit trees to eke out an existence. So the reality of the paradise garden, containing no more than shade trees and cooling water, has, until recently, been unknown.

Improved irrigational techniques and a knowledge of soil improvement

have recently encouraged primarily large-scale planting, in some parts, to screen and shelter new developments and stabilize sand; to establish an ecological system which integrates grazing, farming and forestry; and, in the micro-climate in the lee ʾof this wide-scale afforestation, to allow a more prosperous settled life to emerge, including decorative small-scale planting within the family unit.

Flowers and plants not only feature as an integral part of a miniature, they are also often used to decorate its borders. In this seventeenth-century Mughal miniature of a dervish there are wide and richly decorated borders depicting a variety of plants such as strawberries, violas, anemones and tulips.

THE ISLAMIC GARDEN TODAY AND ITS FUTURE

The gardens and their pavilions whose development we have considered have been mainly palatial, for a ruler and his court have the means to build as they like and the land on which to do so. It is therefore these palatial complexes, usually conceived, as we have seen, according to a precedent but modified according to the location, which have created stylistic developments. But in many parts of the Islamic world, and especially in Arabia, wealth was expressed more in numbers of camels and sheep than in permanent material possessions, and the rich were thus kept on the move to defend their lands and find new grazing. The fixed riches of a palace and garden did not fit into such a scheme of things. Only the discovery of oil in the twentieth century has brought any measure of this kind of wealth, resulting in a more settled life and a standard of living inconceivable for many as little as twenty years ago. This new-found affluence based on Western expertise has led, not unnaturally, to Western influence in the cultural field as well. Yet this new life-style inwardly seeks to achieve some reconciliation with traditional, inherent and indigenous Islam.

Today's rulers of the prosperous Arabian states have little precedent on which to base the creation of their palaces. They still follow indigenous Islamic tradition in having households dotted about their kingdoms, and many still lead the same migratory life between them that their ancestors led between tented encampments, so that in one sense this tradition continues. The complexes are still enclosed and very private – the expression of a twentieth-century paradise. But the outward form of some of the buildings lacks the essence of any tradition which might be passed on to their heirs. Buildings have often been conceived and built by Western architects with little understanding of the culture and only a passing knowledge of the harsh climate.

We have seen how mosques and tomb buildings are often heavily enriched externally, each being built according to a particular concept. The mosque is inward-looking – a place of tranquillity for ritual ablution and prayer. The tomb belongs to a quite different tradition, being positioned centrally in its garden. The palace, however, was a series of pavilions, a complex with each pavilion serving a particular function, the whole welded together as a single concept by water and the necessary shade trees.

The designers of modern palatial buildings have often confused these traditional concepts and, also influenced no doubt by the European tradition of setting a building squarely in the centre of its site, have produced palaces which, like the tomb buildings, are monuments to their inhabitants. The Western idea of an Eastern style is also apparent in the enrichment and decoration of such buildings, which, constructed for secular use, have little precedent in the Middle East.

The recently completed campus of the Sultan Qaboos University at Muscat, Oman, designed by YRM International/Brian Clouston and Partners, is a fine contemporary example of the re-interpretation of basic Islamic garden principles.

A modern enclosed garden in the foothills outside Muscat, Oman.

We in the West are perhaps privileged to be seeing only the beginning of a new interchange of cultural ideas with this part of the world – for in the past Islam infused much into European thinking; however, let the return match now be played in technology alone, so that the future concept of building in the Middle East takes on its own regional identity once more.

The recent higher standard of living – again in Western terms – has led to the development of new towns and cities, or the enlarging of old ones. Within these schemes, the private dwelling makes up a major part, along with hospitals, schools and universities. Interestingly, the large modern campus layout lends itself well to the adaptation of an Islamic form of pavilion-in-a-garden landscape. Indeed, the European tradition of a university quadrangle is a descendant of the monastic cloister, which in its turn is derived from Islam through Moorish Spain. But smaller housing units do not always fare so well. Again often conceived on the Western drawing board, the concept of cheek-by-jowl living is alien to this part of the world. The hustle and bustle of the bazaar or souk is accepted, but home life must be enclosed and private, centring on the courtyard. Families too, within the home, are larger and the traditional home plan allows far greater flexibility, for much of life can be led outside or in the shade of surrounding buildings. The solution to this growing complexity of living and life-style, therefore, is not to be found in the Western example of the house centred on its site, with a grassed garden front and rear, allowing for a display of worldly trappings.

IRAN TODAY

Iran today, in principal urban areas at least, presents a parallel with the burgeoning prosperity of much of the Middle East. It is sad that, with such a history, many Iranian gardens owe so little in their layout to their Islamic tradition. It seems that those people who are actively involved in garden-making are the very ones who seek to reject this past, and who project themselves into twentieth-century, Western ways of living. The reasons for this lie in the fact that Iran has a vast rural population and few urban centres. In these centres a rich minority sponsored by the former regime of the shah sought to lead the country into a form of twentieth-century industrialization. Such a process inevitably depopulated what had been a thriving agricultural environment which was left to revert, in many cases, to desert, with life-giving *qanats* allowed to become blocked up or to collapse. The affluent minority rejected the old traditional Persian ways, completed their education or took holidays in Europe or the United States and not surprisingly imported into Iran an alien western life-style. Of course, this Westernization had to be transported into Iranian terms of reference, one of which was Shii Islam and another the large family unit, for Iranian households include not only grandparents but often many other close relations and servants as well.

The household is therefore a substantial unit in its own right, and the garden to it has necessarily huge demands made upon it – for while the house may be large, the garden space, in a town anyway, often is not. Parking for three or four cars may well be needed, and hanging space for airing clothes, a play space and, of course, a swimming pool. Wide terraces adjoin the house, too, for summer evening entertaining. The Iranian garden now is very definitely a place for active use – no longer for restful contemplation, to be viewed from a pavilion while reclining on cushions –

and yet it could retain some essence of this traditional function, if the Persian desire for outward show did not lead to over-complication with Japanese lanterns, Italian balustrading, Californian garden seating and continental spot planting of shrubs in grass.

Such a confusion is understandable, for the middle-class urban home and twentieth-century building style has little precedent, but slowly an awareness and interest in rural vernacular architecture is growing, which varies considerably throughout the country and which one hopes will imbue future development with a far greater sense of indigenous style, leading also to greater garden simplicity. A rise in the cost of labour will ensure that the garden is not left to the whims of the gardener, who tends to make work for himself, but to the owner taking a greater interest in his own plot. Let us hope that any such interest will not become too horticultural in aspect (the ubiquitous blue conifer has started to make its glaucous appearance already). There is still a great love of plants in Iran – witness the trees, shrubs and annuals sold at many urban street corners – but their use in any aesthetic sense has not yet been learnt, nor surprisingly has the desire to grow one's own produce. The fruit trees of the *chahar bagh* were obviously a practical necessity; now there is an apparently endless supply of cheap fruit and vegetables in shops and the bazaar, and produce in the main is not home-grown.

ABOVE *A spacious house in north Tehran, Iran, with all the requisites of a modern home – garage, driveway and a garden shaded by large weeping willows.*

207

Magnificent new parks are now starting to mature in the major cities, and the techniques which have been used in their design (ground-cover planting, for instance, bold shrub and tree groupings and broad masses of grass) could point a way towards greater simplicity. It is perhaps from park layouts, where the traditional elements of the Persian garden are being re-introduced, that much can be learnt. Cool streams of water flow near shaded lawns while gentle fountains play nearby. Such places are heavily used, from the first light of morning to the cool of the evening.

Greater consideration of design for use rather than for show might make the average Iranian garden more practical and far easier to maintain. Having said this, one does not want to apply Western gardening techniques as a criterion, for gardening as we in the West know it really has little relevance in the Middle East. Conversely, an awareness of nature and what it has to offer – its coolness, its flowers, greenery and fruits – is highly developed in Iran. These aspects have been praised and evoked in metaphor from the Quran onwards: in literature, in poetry, in carpet weaving, in miniatures – and even in revolutionary slogans.

So much in climate as well as in use differs from the Western ideal; nevertheless, where a domestic garden is attempted, it seems that much could be simplified and other indigenous aspects developed to make Persian gardens more Persian again. In Iran, grass is necessarily a luxury and needs constant watering during summer. European gardens, particularly in England, tend to be constructed basically of a lawn, with areas of planting and water and anything else imposed on the background medium of grass. This is not so in the Middle East, where the basic medium is dust; so grass is another 'special' planted medium and is treated as such.

A major feature of Iranian gardens is shade, originally given by rows of fruit trees in the *chahar bagh*. This practice has now given way to random planting in grass of deciduous specimens – shrubs as well as trees – so that differing heights and levels, some giving shade and some reaching to the ground, give an unrestful, arboretum-like feel to what should be a simple green canopy. The traditional chenar alone, with its lower branches removed, gives a lovely shade, its blotched stems making a sculptural addition to the garden throughout the year. The individual specimen shade tree, such as the fig, catalpa, acacia or palm, is not made enough of either, whether in garden or courtyard.

These days the swimming pool seems to dominate the average urban

OPPOSITE ABOVE *A public park in the foothills of the Alborz mountains in north Tehran, Iran. Wide flights of steps, bordered by shade-giving trees and split down the middle by canals, culminate in a formal water parterre.*

OPPOSITE BELOW *A channel of rushing water in a modern Tehran park still provides the timeless qualities of refreshment and enjoyment.*

garden, and in the height of summer it is very necessary; too often, however, one suspects it is there as an expensive status symbol and not as a useful addition, for it is apparent that the new owner does not realize the amount of enforced daily care which is necessary to maintain a pool to a usable standard. Further, that same pool may well dominate the garden; often it is the only view one has from October until the following May, and during all that time it lies there, an empty chasm in the layout.

When the pool *is* used the areas of hard surfacing around it are often too small for family use, and the ratio of water to paved surround is incorrect. If the pool were accepted as a water tank in the traditional sense, and its outline simplified, it could fit more easily into an overall symmetrical plan without dominating the whole. Symmetry is needed for such a layout and this must also flow on from the traditional house layout with its *talar* and terrace. Again, the pursuit of the Western ideal in modern, modish Iranian architecture has produced 'clever' asymmetry which is difficult to accommodate in the garden scheme.

But now there is a welcome reappraisal of traditional Persian forms and materials. Hand in hand with this has gone a re-examination of the use of

Like the traditional water tank the modern swimming pool makes a harmonious addition to a late nineteenth-century courtyard home in Muscat, Oman. The pool is completely shaded by lattice against the intense heat of the sun.

the home. It should be appreciated that it is probably only in the last fifty years that the chair, for instance, has been used in Iran – and it still has no place in many rural homes. Life was extremely simple – one sat on a carpet and, later, bedding was unrolled upon it and the family slept there, then it was put away next day. Food and pots were kept on shelves around the room; and there were hangings on the wall. While the house was still the focal point of the home, it was far less lived in than in the West, and in the summer this same style of living was continued out of doors under shade. This was a fairly basic way of living which in an even more primitive form is still carried on by tribal peoples in the desert under tents. Somewhere between this basic form and the Hollywood fantasies of the 1960s and 1970s there must be an Iranian ideal for both indoors and out.

THE FUTURE

What happens next in the Middle East? If not in Arabia, certainly in other parts of the Middle East, civilizations have come and gone. Are we witnessing in Saudi Arabia and in the Gulf States the emergence of a new life-style, still Islamic, but more militant, a flexing of muscles – a rejuvenation? Politically this may be so, but what of the landscape and the concept of paradise within it?

As water is the key to life in the desert, and the continuing theme throughout this book, future development of the dry lands of the Middle East must depend on it too. So, when looking towards the future, one has to look at water usage in broad terms to make any development possible at all. Irrigational methods are the key to this step forward, so long as water sources are assured and its usage is not to the detriment of the country at large. Adequate drainage facilities, too, are necessary, for even in a hot climate increasingly fertile soils can become waterlogged and eventually saline. This is still an unresolved problem and one which was a contributing factor to the downfall of great civilizations in both the Tigris and Euphrates valleys. Future methods of irrigation will determine future landscape patterns.

In the wider landscape where there is considerable afforestation, desert reclamation and subsequent crop production are starting, and larger-scale forms of water distribution are necessary; and it is these which are altering the Middle Eastern landscape so dramatically in parts.

With improved irrigational techniques the Quranic conception of the paradisiacal enclosure as a retreat from the hostility of the surrounding landscape becomes obsolete for, with water, whole new regions may now become green and fertile. Yet, conversely, the prosperity that fosters this rejuvenation of the landscape must also foster development within it – the provision of public open spaces for parks, incidental play areas of green, and the idealized or tamed form of nature which we call the garden. And no matter how green the landscape or how fertile the fields, the sun will be as hot, and the ever-present need for shade for man – the user of the landscape – does not change physically, and his requirements will still be the same, though possibly on a smaller scale, as those of earlier garden-makers within Islam.

To escape the teeming streets, the bazaars and the souks, and to refresh himself, traditional man sought out the tea house, the bath and the quiet privacy of his family, his inward-looking courtyard and its surrounding home. Such an ideal must still be attainable, indeed is more urgent than ever, for the virtues of Islamic home life may still provide a change of pace from the clamour of public life to the calm of the private one. And the centre of this can still be the garden for, outwardly at least, shade and water and the peace which they engender can still provide an even more necessary earthly paradise and some escape from the hurly-burly of twentieth-century living.

NOTES ON DESIGNING A GARDEN IN THE MIDDLE EAST

LIMITATIONS OF A DESERT CLIMATE

In considering how the ideal of the Islamic garden can be achieved in the Middle East today, it is necessary to take into account the limitations imposed by the climate. With improving technology much can be done to alleviate the rigours of Arabia and its Gulf; better irrigational methods have recently altered the landscape considerably, turning what was an arid waste into a productive and green landscape. But in general the climate, on which water availability depends, is still a harsh unchanging factor in this part of the world, and will shape the life of all who tread its wastes. In the lush green areas of the Western world, we are fortunate to live *in* the *favourable* landscapes which surround us as part of a total and natural life-cycle. In the Middle East, one is all too conscious of living *on* an *unfavourable* landscape, which has to be known and manipulated to support a knife-edge existence.

TEMPERATURE

During summer the sun beats down unmercifully, and the temperatures reached are often far higher than those at the Equator. Maximum day temperatures may reach 37° to 47°C and temperatures of over 52°C are known. In parts of both Saudi Arabia and Iran one may experience some of the highest temperatures in the world.

Autumn and spring are short; spring weather is changeable, while autumn is pleasant, warm and sunny. In winter, however, although frost is unusual at sea level, the interior can become very cold, especially on higher ground. Snow can fall as far south as the Yemen and southern Iran, precipitated by the mountain ranges, so that extremes throughout the year can vary between freezing point and 47°C (in London the average range is 15°C).

WIND

Sand- and salt-laden winds blow continually in the desert. They may not only cause great damage by their persistent force, but the dust which they carry has a blasting effect; they are also dehydrating. One virtue of the traditional enclosed building is to deflect these winds over the house and courtyard which it encloses. The tightly knit complex of buildings in a traditional town or village provided a way of achieving the same end.

At certain times of year, the wind builds up to dust storms, known in the Gulf States as *shamals*, and when blowing with full force they can knock a man over. They usually begin quite innocuously as dust devils – whirling spirals of sand which dance over the ground and are caused by loose dust, often churned up by a vehicle or a horse. This results in the hot air rising and cooler air circulating down to replace it, thereby generating the typical swirl which picks up debris and dust as it moves along. In rotation the dust particles give off more heat, causing rapidly rising air to feed more dust to the devil, which at a certain point turns into a *shamal. Shamals* occur mostly in the spring. An obvious limiting factor to these forceful, dust-laden winds is the stabilization of areas of loose sand.

RAINFALL

The irregularity and scantiness of rainfall is really the major limiting factor in this part of the world. In some areas years may go by without any substantial rain at all, while in others there are deluges for a short spell, causing flooding and the characteristic, deeply scored landscape, but the largest areas of the Middle East are dry, definable if not as zones of extreme desert aridity, at least as arid. Some sources maintain that any area which gets less than 350 mm of rain annually is a desert. Others state that only those areas which receive less than 100 mm can be called deserts, and that areas with more rain, 100 up to 500 mm, are arid or semi-arid. By either definition, the greater part of Arabia/Saudi Arabia is one of the harshest desert landscapes in the world; large areas of Iran fit into this category as well.

When rain does fall in the desert, only approximately 10 per cent goes into the soil, and that percolates to only a very shallow depth. Twenty per cent is used in wetting the surface of the ground alone, and 20 per cent more evaporates almost immediately as a result of intense solar radiation, stored heat and wind. The remaining 50 per cent runs off, to evaporate in wadis, and it is only this 50 per cent which is even potentially collectable for future use. In the Saudi Arabian desert there is usually some rain in most of the winter months from November to April, though the greater amounts fall at the beginning of the year, thus allowing for seed germination. It is the subsequent plant population which provides the essential link in the food chain between the sun's energy and the ability of man and his animals to survive. But it is not surprising that the range of plants which can both survive without irrigation and withstand the onslaught of migrant sheep and goats is limited.

The presence of oases usually denotes an underground water store held by water-bearing rock. Some underground water reserves, or aquifers, have been discovered coincidentally in the search for oil, but large areas of Saudi Arabia may hold as yet undiscovered sources of water. It is not known when aquifers were formed, nor how readily they fill and over what period, but obviously those which are fed by a wadi are more likely to be replaced. However, what is important, particularly in Saudi, is the rate at which aquifers are being tapped. It is imperative that they should be treated as a natural resource of the country as a whole, and not just for the benefit of each individual project. A system of monitoring water extraction should be rigorously imposed, since to draw large quantities of water from non-rechargeable sources is madness, and there is no reason to believe that aquifers can be naturally recharged. There is also the danger that, where underground water is not being recharged, the ground above it may sink; the resultant catastrophe, if an urban area lies above it, can be imagined. Water pressures within the aquifer must therefore be maintained and buildings above them supported. Since it is impossible to store water in the desert, where, exposed to sun and wind, it will quickly evaporate, it should be possible to re-introduce water from wadis, when they are active, into diminishing aquifers, in order that water pressures are maintained in these invaluable underground storage tanks.

The availability of moisture to life, plant or human, in the Arabian peninsula is therefore variable, depending not only on rain, but also on dew and humidity. The extremes of southern and eastern Arabia catch the edge of the monsoon current from the Indian Ocean, increasing their humidity, and they have summer rainfall too. Parts of Oman and the Yemen are also affected in this way. Some upland areas in these parts are therefore amazingly green, supporting a variety of plant and animal life, as in Jordan, Lebanon, western Syria and the higher parts of the North African mountain zone. Northern Iran has a humid jungle bordering the Caspian Sea, and is very similar in fact to parts of the Far East.

SOIL

The study of soil and the relationship between the sparse Gulf soils and the wind, sun and rainfall, and water in general, are manifold and complex. Much has still to be discovered, but the potential cost of ignoring what little is known is massive, and in direct proportion to the size of the Gulf's building programme. It is imperative, therefore, that soil conservation be an integral part of any development programme on whatever scale.

The soils in the Arabian Gulf vary widely from place to place. There are vast areas of sand and equally large areas of exposed natural rock, boulders, pebbles and even natural cement called *hammada*. The soils in oases in the eastern provinces of the area range from sandy-clay loam, to sandy loam, to sand alone. All are quite shallow. The soil in the mountains and in Yemen benefits from increased rainfall and the ensuing plant growth enriches it, even where there is no cultivation of it by man. Where alluvial deposits collect, as in wadi bottoms, soil is often fairly deep and, because of the increased moisture available, plant growth is encouraged; this in turn encourages the development of better, more fertile soil. There are also other soils of volcanic origin.

However, much soil in Saudi Arabia is of recent deposit, forming a shallow layer over ground rock, or some sort of hardpan. In many places, especially the great sandy areas, the wind causes massive shifts of local soil, in this case sand, from one place to another, but shifting dunes and shifting soils also include clay and silt in some parts of the desert. Wherever there is enough loose soil to take part in such massive movements, it has to be stabilized with plant cover before any development can take place.

Even accumulations of mature soil are dispersed by the wind when they lack sufficient vegetation to hold them in place. The combined effects of wind and run-off constantly redistributing the soil make even relatively recent soil descriptions unreliable on the basis of geological conditions.

For this reason most desert soils have not matured and are highly alkaline when compared to temperate soils, which are neutral or acid. The alkalinity of desert soils is responsible for the formation of hardpan. Often exposed by wind (as in the *hammadas*), hardpan is a cement of gravel and cobbles mortared together by salts, leached from above, and lime, eroded from bedrock below. It causes poor drainage in many soils, which also develop impermeable surface salt crusts, thus promoting water run-off. This situation can also occur where soils are underlaid by clay.

There are four main types of desert soil:

1   *Hammada* soils which, as we have seen, are poor and hard and therefore difficult to cultivate. They are made up of a stony medium and only support a very small range of plants naturally.

2   Sand dunes, whose hazard is their mobility in the wind and the possibility of their encroaching on neighbouring better soils. They are produced by the action of wind on sand and silt particles. According to the volume of silt in the dune, sand will vary in its ability to allow water to drain: the higher the silt content, the lower the absorption rate, but the more stable and less likely to move it is.

3   Loess soil, which is fine-grained, semi-heavy and potentially fertile. However, it is liable to crumble to dust when dry, and under rain or irrigation it forms a hard impenetrable crust which causes surface water to collect in flash floods, which in turn create boggy conditions. Characteristic gulleying occurs, caused by excessive water run-off.

4   Brackish soils, which in many cases consist of two types of soil appear-
     ing together. They frequently have a high degree of salinity.

The soil in the desert also has high concentrations of sodium, potassium
and calcium. The high sodium content is apparently counteracted by the
high calcium concentration, and so does not inhibit plant growth. But the
potassium and calcium, and other essential elements such as manganese,
iron, boron, and sulphur, are seldom available to plants growing in it
because of the lack of moisture and organic activity in the soil. Certain of
these elements in Saudi soils exist in the form of salts which may be
harmful to plants in excess. Magnesium salts for instance inhibit chloro-
phyll production, and sulphur salts are harmful to plants in other ways.
Even in relatively fertile parts of the desert where nutrients exist in usable
form and in the correct concentrations, they are usually confined to the
top five or ten centimetres of soil. But where irrigation systems are in use,
pumping ground water on to land in an area of these elemental salt build-
ups (and because soil and ground water in the same location have similar
properties and pH values), the end result can be often only to aggravate
the situation by a greater build-up of salts. For this reason plans are under
way to treat the ground water in order to leach or drain out the
harmful substances. But on practical and economic grounds this leaching
is seldom the most feasible way to deal with harmful concentrations of
elements in the soil.

The long-term key to changing the make-up of desert soils, so that they
can support useful vegetation, is not irrigation or leaching or the inclusion
of peat moss or chemical fertilizers. It is quite simply vegetation and the
underground organic activity that vegetation creates. There is a precedent
for improving soil by a succession of 'crops', or green manures, which in
temperate climates are ploughed into the ground. In the desert dead plants
should not be ploughed into the soil but should be allowed to fall to the
ground, bake, decay and be absorbed into the soil. The crops' roots and
the microbes which co-exist with them will continue to develop soil below
the surface. The ability of deserts to support vegetation can be greatly
enhanced in this way, under cultivation purposefully planned to improve
the soil, sometimes even without the need for irrigation. These techniques
are time-honoured soil- and water-conservation measures which, while
bearing greater fruits eventually, are often not practised on large-scale

developments, since quicker results are now generally required. Water alone may 'improve' the desert in some areas, but only on a short-term basis.

SURFACES

When considering larger horizontal surfaces in the Islamic world, one is beginning to explore new ground, for while pattern is a great part of the decoration of vertical surfaces – in tiling, timberwork and stone carving, and on a smaller scale to cover fabrics, manuscripts and the floors of interiors – the tradition has not been to pave public open spaces. Rather, richness of pattern has been reserved for areas of more private, intimate pleasure, where paved patterns would have been subordinate to the general one of pools and fountains.

Public open spaces like the piazzas of Renaissance Italy are few. The *maydan* in Isfahan is perhaps the open area most closely comparable. This was once surfaced in gravel and used as a polo pitch or market area. Would that it were now – for the current municipal-garden approach is totally incorrect; the garden lay through Ali Qapu, the heavenly gate between the hardness of the public world and the softness of the shah's private paradise garden beyond.

Public open spaces which exist on any large scale are to be found within the mosque courtyard or tomb surround. It is arguable that this *is* the Muslim public open space – a descendant of the Roman forum – and here there are some examples of fine hard surfacing, but they are few. Physical conditions in Arabia no doubt contributed to this lack of secular public open space: the wind, frequently localized, encouraged the traditional use of enclosing elements to counteract and restrict wind flow; the ever-present overhead sun dictated the need for shade. Most mosque courtyards, it will be seen, are surrounded by a shaded colonnade.

Associated with open spaces too is the problem of glare. Glare can of course occur from any direction, relative to the sun's position, and the vertical elements surrounding a paved area are as likely to induce it as the horizontal one between them. The problem of glare comprises three elements – brightness, contrast and reflection. The use of matt surfaces, rich colours and, of course, shade will counteract these. Careful selection of ground materials in both colour and texture is therefore essential to reduce this, along with a constant awareness of scale. Planting can do much to break up large areas of open space, and can of course alleviate other problems. It is difficult to believe – for the Western reader anyway – that one of these is rain! We have already seen that large areas have very little, but when it does rain, it rains hard, and in some areas it is of monsoon intensity. Traditional Western forms of drainage to underground pipes cannot cope with a sudden onslaught, particularly when not in regular use, since they are so easily blocked with wind-blown sand. This means that quick drainage to an open system of water escape is vital if a major flood is to be avoided. The raised walks of the *chahar bagh* in Persia and India are built this way for that very reason.

It is not often realized that until comparatively recently most external ground surfaces were porous, and therefore permitted water to drain away. But the tremendous increase in hard impervious ground-covering in new developments, coupled with a similar increase in built-up areas in which people now live, has led directly to a much higher likelihood of serious flood damage, because the surface layers of sand are so compacted by vehicular weight. The consolidated granular gravel, or chipping, traditionally used for surfacing large areas, encouraged natural drainage, while the other material used for surfacing was simple squares of cut stone slabs, varying in size according to the skills and materials available. To a lesser degree, hand-made clay bricks were used for small-scale decorative areas and, for even more special ones, as in the mosque courtyard, cut marble. In India the patterned marble floorings round the Taj Mahal are exquisite and amazingly cool in full sun as one walks barefoot across them.

Modern pavings which are available for use in the Middle East will be of standard concrete proportions, the larger slab or smaller tile, but it should be remembered that the chemical conditions already described in the soil may well affect anything laid upon it, and there might well be a build-up of salts, leading to a chemical reaction on contact with metals, concrete and certain natural stones. The use of sulphate-resisting concrete is normally recommended for use as a paving constituent. The source of the aggregate supply and its chemical and weathering characteristics should also be checked. Washing in pure water is often the only way to achieve suitable standards and this in itself can create problems. Many of these factors make it preferable to use a dry construction and a reliable natural stone for paved areas.

Brickwork as a flooring medium might also be liable to salt attack, but the small-scale patterns which can be created in brick, or brick combined with another medium, are of a scale very much in the Islamic tradition and in an area which is viewed and appreciated from above can be even more dramatic. The differing porosity of available bricks according to their firing will also affect their heat-retention properties: that is, the harder the finish, the more heat will be deflected rather than held. The most readily available bricks, however, are made of clay and are sun-dried on the spot.

The Western designer evolving Islamic patterns on his drawing board might also bear in mind that there is no craft tradition of laying pavings in the Middle East, and this could prove yet another problem.

GARDEN LAYOUT

The design of a garden in the Middle East will depend very much on the household which it serves, its form, whether traditional or modern, being determined by the design of the building which surrounds it. That its concept, for very practical reasons, should be Islamic, should be apparent by now, although the desire to re-create a European lushness is understandable. Many aspects of the European tradition *will* travel, but it should be realized that their introduction is in opposition to the natural characteristics of the site; the most fitting garden, therefore, will conform to its surroundings and become an idealized form of what already exists.

Having said that, one has to allow for the presence of factors more typical of a Western style of living: car parking, access to services, a rubbish enclosure, a swimming pool, and a children's area, amongst other things. However, these are merely the practical requirements of the site, around which a design is evolved. It is important when planning a garden to be aware of these aspects at the outset, for they are as much a part of the garden as the trees and plants which will bind the whole design together.

The garden then should very much reflect the life-style of its owners; it will ultimately be much more beautiful and successful if it 'works' for them too. Like a suit of clothing, it has to be cut to fit both the life-style and the pocket of the wearer. So evolve a simple ground pattern first of all, allowing plenty of space for access paths for your vehicles and for visitors and services to and from the house. Then in the mind's eye connect up the other elements of the garden for a logical progression round the site, bearing in mind the need for shade, for wind shelter, for watering facilities and for surfaces which will not be too glaring or retain the heat. Consider the views you will get from all parts of the house into the area, as well as those when in the garden. Consider night-time as well as day. Think of the noise from children in a play area, or from teenagers round a swimming pool. Where will you sit in the cool of the evening and what will you see?

Sites might have been larger and times more gracious and less technical during the period of the historical gardens which we have looked at, but broadly the demands of the garden then were not dissimilar to those now. The fact that they worked for the household or court which used them is evident in that they still exist. For an unused or misused garden soon deteriorates. Unlike a building, which is static, a garden continuously grows. To accommodate this natural movement its style should 'fit' as well, for the garden used for enjoyment is the Quranic ideal of paradise, as apt now as when first described.

Having established a practical outline for the garden's functions, and a landscape designer will always help if necessary, it is time to start considering its planting – and the process works in that order!

The limitations of plant growth in the Middle East are legion. Many plants have adapted themselves naturally to high temperatures, to lack of water or to strong winds, but for garden use many of these indigenous species are not particularly attractive for that very reason – they are little more than scrub coverage. Shrubs tend to be spiny and scruffy in appearance, with insignificant flowers and little physical beauty. The herb layer consists largely of tufted grasses or flowering annuals with an extremely short life-cycle. Added to the rigours of climate are the problems of grazing animals, for herds of sheep and goats often seem as common in the centre of town as they are in the surrounding desert.

Although natural desert growth often seems intermittent if it exists at all, the root runs of certain plants can be enormous in order to gather up as much moisture as possible, so the smaller shrub can in fact be stabilizing the ground over quite a large area. It is amazing too, after the lightest rain, to discover how much has been lying dormant in a seemingly lifeless waste, and to watch it come briefly to life. While much can be learnt from the ecology and natural plant cycles of the desert in the Middle East, it has little relevance as a guide to plant selection on the domestic scale, so one seeks to extend the plant vocabulary to provide a far wider range of exotics, to include colourful shrubs and trees which are capable of providing shelter and shade.

Whatever the chosen form of planting, the need for adequate water and watering facilities for growth, in almost any situation, cannot be overemphasized, for once water application has started, it must be consistent for growth to continue. Under dry conditions, plants have well-developed defences against water loss. If water application starts, this defence system deteriorates, and the interruption of watering can have fatal consequences. Given water, which must not be applied without attention to its quality and to the characteristics of the soil and its feeding, extraordinary growth rates can be produced of up to two metres per season, both upwards and outwards.

The question of what will grow where will also be influenced by latitude, altitude and the proximity to the sea. The enormous climatic differences in the Middle East prohibit the listing of suitable plants, but the following outline factors should be considered when making a selection. (One limiting factor, of course, must be what is available to buy in this comparatively new market. It is probably safe to assume, however, that what is available locally will grow, since it is in the interest of the supplier to ensure this.)

When starting to think of plants for the garden to infill the basic plan, each category and size of plant should be considered one at a time, from the largest down to the smallest. Firstly trees are needed to provide shelter from the wind, to block some views and emphasize others. Specimen trees can be sited for special effect – for shade, for flower or fruit. Next, large-scale intentions should be reinforced with tall infill shrubs, using this grouping as the background planting for more interesting smaller ones. Plants should be selected not only for their flower colour but for leaf colour as well: the shades of green are many and varied, according to the leaf form. Texture is important as well. Try to visualize the result in, say, five years' time, so that mentally you compose a grouping. Do not be wooed into trying too many different species, since the end result may well be unrestful – each plant does not have to differ from its neighbour. Conversely, plant shade trees in a grove all of one type. To decide which sort of tree you want, it is helpful to envisage the shape and particular leaf form each will give you, and the sort of canopy that the trees together will create – a light, dappled shade or a heavy, dark one.

Romantic though the image of foliage hanging into water may be, remember that you will have to have such water cleaned even more often than usual. Sheets of water used decoratively in a hot climate, whether in pools or canals, need to be kept moving or constantly recirculating to avoid the very rapid build-up of green algae and cloudiness of the water that will otherwise take place. For it is the crystal clarity of water, used in whatever form, which evokes the sensation of coolness.

Lastly, accept where you are in the world – by all means improve on nature, but do not try to re-create what was seen on holiday or on a business trip in some other part of the world. The chances are that without untold effort it will not work for you.

SOIL PREPARATION AND IMPROVEMENT

Before considering any sort of planting in any soil type, some preparation of the ground is necessary. The removal of stones from the site is fairly obvious – then, where possible, the improvement of the soil by the addition of organic matter to it, for desert soils are sorely lacking in this. Organic manure is, however, scarce and landscape firms embarking on large projects have even imported buffalo dung from as far as India to provide it. On newer developments the availability of sewage sludge which has undergone some degree of treatment might be explored. Unpleasant smell is an obvious by-product of its use, for which reason it should be dug or ploughed in as soon as possible. It will provide a basis for vital organisms in the soil to become activated and will also help to retain moisture.

Another way of providing organic content is to sow a 'green manure' of, say, Rhodos grass and *Lolium* spp. in early winter with the addition of a nitrogenous fertilizer, and then turn it into the ground the following spring before planting.

A simple form of irrigation must then be considered, for the traditional form of surface irrigation or hand watering on a small scale is very wasteful of water. It should be appreciated that a growing tree will need some ten gallons of water per day, depending on the season, its size, etc. Both trees and shrubs should be watered by a system of trickle supply, with water dripping from a nozzle sited adjacent to the tree and running at a very low rate. As long as the water is applied to the soil surface exactly where it is needed, there is very little evaporation loss. It has been estimated that this system will use approximately 66 per cent of the amount of water that a sprinkler system will use, and only 40 per cent of the water of a surface watering system. There are various controlling devices to monitor the system, which can be continuous round a whole garden, so that it is possible to maintain almost any required moisture regime.

Sprinkler systems are more extravagant with water, as there is a larger evaporation loss. Efficiency can be reduced in high winds, too, and in combination with the invariably strong sunlight there is a risk of scorching the leaves of the plants being watered. Night-time watering can overcome this, of course. However, over areas of lawn the sprinkler system is ideal. It is installed under the area to be watered, with the nozzles placed so that they are flush or just below ground level. When the water supply is turned on the pressure in the supply makes the sprinklers rise clear of the ground, allowing an uninterrupted range for irrigation. These pop-up nozzles retreat when the water is turned off so as not to impede surface mowing.

GRASS

Of all the growing materials in a landscape, grass is the most emotive, for the broad swards of it seen in the European landscape form a natural ground coverage. This is not so in the Middle East; while a lawn can be achieved, it is not without great effort and labour cost. Water will have to be used extravagantly (thirty litres per square metre per day, even by sprinkler technique) and between a third and a half of the water will evaporate before it reaches the plants' roots.

Grass species should be of the rhizome type, of which the following are the most commonly successful: *Cynodon dactylon* (Bermuda type),

Stenotaphrum secundatum and *Pennisetum clandestinum*. Lawns should be planted in drills 50–100 mm deep and 150 mm apart, with each drill filled continuously with grass rhizomes 400 mm long. The rhizomes are covered with soil to allow only 40 mm of the upper foliage to remain above ground level. After planting, the area is either rolled or trodden over, and irrigation should be carried out immediately.

With all the work of establishing a lawn, it remains the only soft surfacing which will withstand heavy usage, so where the garden is primarily for use, particularly by children, it cannot be bettered. Ground-covering plants can also be used to infill large areas where a soft finish is required, but they will not withstand any wear. However, they do have the advantage of flowering, and many of the succulents which store water in their leaves or have underground tubers for that reason are most decorative and much easier to look after, needing no mowing either. Succulent ground cover should, however, be in full sun in the main, though grass may have trees planted through it and will be quite happy in light shade.

TREES

In the harsh new developments which are increasing at an enormous rate in the Middle East, the need for trees is paramount. For the luxury of vegetation not only softens new buildings, but provides shelter from wind when used peripherally, and shelter from sun in all vehicular parking areas, between houses and over public and private open spaces. In short, trees can temper the whole life-style.

Traditionally, the date palm provided a major contribution to food supply and in the arid areas of Arabia was the only major vegetation occurring round oases. Further north and higher up, deciduous fruit trees have replaced the palm in greater variety – the almond, pistachio nut, apricot, pomegranate and peach. On the high plateau of Iran, plums, apples, pears and walnuts grow before the land drops down to the orange groves of the Caspian seaboard. In Kashmir the apple orchards are famed, along with groves of walnut trees. On the hot plains in India the mango, paw-paw and banana abound, so the Islamic tradition of fruit trees within the garden is maintained. Increasingly, however, urban planting in Saudi Arabia and the Gulf States is of decorative species of tree, often nonindigenous and needing more care and attention when newly planted than do native species.

Drip irrigation is the efficient way of watering trees as it is directed where it is needed. Indigenous trees such as tamarisk, acacia, zaizyphus and prosopis will grow with little water initially. Decorative species such as eucalyptus, casuarina or schinus will need permanent irrigation for the first five years after being planted.

The investment in trees, in labour and water resources, is therefore considerable, and it would seem sensible to ensure that when they mature there is some return on the investment, by way of fruit or ultimately timber. Ideally, too, the trees should go some way to improving the fertility of the soil, alongside their decorative function. This might seem much to expect, but a considerable number of species can fulfil at least some of these criteria in some places. They would seem a better long-term investment, too, than the large-scale planting of more spectacular alien introductions which need specialist knowledge of their particular requirements, since at this stage the desert environment is still being modified. The basic requirements are therefore: trees that can resist heat, drought and wind; trees that are resistant to some degree of salinity in the soil; trees for urban and domestic use that are economic as well as ornamental; and trees that are indigenous to climatic conditions not too far removed from those in which they are to be planted.

When planting trees, it is essential to give them a good start, preparing a pit for each one at least one metre square and one metre deep. This should be filled with water at least twice to allow the surrounding ground maximum absorption. Then prepare a layer of sweet wadi soil, or soil and organic waste, at least 400 mm deep at the bottom of the hole. Trees are usually bought contained in an old tin, in which they should be well watered before being placed in the hole prepared for them. Cut down the sides of the tin so that it can be carefully slipped from underneath the roots without disturbing them or the soil surrounding them. If there is not a sufficient matrix of root around the ball of the tree a wire-netting container may be made round them, before the pit is backfilled and firmed. They should then be watered again, before the normal programme of irrigational watering is begun. Date palms should have their trunks protected with burlap; some would recommend frond wrapping with hessian as well, which should remain in place for two growing seasons. Trees are planted in November and December, although date palms are planted between June and August.

SHRUBS

The shrubs and roses which you select will provide the colour necessary in your layout and also the visual link between overhead trees and ground cover. Shrubs grow quickly when watered and their roots bind the soil in an open, exposed situation. There are many leguminous types of shrub (that is, those which belong to the pea family) which are suited to arid conditions and have a root system which contributes to soil fertility. Shrubs too can be used to divide the garden and provide either a loose hedge or, if clipped (the correct types, that is), a formal one, although this usually precludes their flowering.

At this stage, then, along with the use of perennials and herbaceous material, colour should be considered, just as one might devise a scheme for the inside of the house. In the dry parts of the world plants occur naturally in communities of a limited number of species, having adapted themselves for that particular situation. Generally, the uniform scale of growth and type is what characterizes the community, and unity of colour is of secondary importance. In the urban domestic situation of a desert climate, and often as a refuge from the broad barren areas of surrounding landscape and wide hot horizons, the eye seeks tranquillity in deep glades of shade with broad areas of cool water and large drifts of colour to accompany it – although this is a recent innovation in the Middle East. And in association with the clean lines of new developments and the mass of a blue-lined swimming pool, colour groupings should all be to scale. The small salt-and-pepper effect of the English cottage garden has no place in this scale of landscape.

Such sweeping analysis obviously has it flaws, but it is not a bad premise from which to start when considering this aspect of garden design. Colours too can be strong in sunlight, since much of their intensity is 'soaked up' by the sun, although in shade cool colours and those of deeper intensity will extend the mood. If one accepts this premise, use drifts of colour blending one with another as a progression. One does not need to be shocked by violent colour clashes.

The value of scent in the garden in a hot climate cannot be overemphasized, and it is one of the most evocative aspects of the Islamic garden concept: not only the smell of flowers and foliage, but of moisture as well, of wet grass and even hard surfaces when watered. As the temperature increases scents come alive: and in the traditional enclosure – a place of still air – when the family takes its evening meal outside, the scent should hang heavy and offer a further balm, along with the sound of water, to the hot night air.

Shade can be provided both by buildings and the canopy which trees can create. However, a transitional stage between the shade of a building and the shade from a tree is that provided by the creeper-clad canopy or pergola – a green form of the arcade. A great virtue of many climbers or creepers is that, during the cooler months of winter when it is desirable to have some sunshine percolating through the structure which supports them, the plants themselves are at their most feeble, allowing it to filter through. During the growing season, however, the rate of growth, with adequate water, is phenomenal.

Climbers can also be used for screening boundaries and softening them, for losing tennis-court surrounds, although the netting through which they can be grown should be reinforced, since they become very heavy. They can also be allowed to ramble across the ground and thus provide a very useful and colourful ground medium, actually creeping on to the beach at times, while still flourishing.

SUCCULENTS

Perhaps understandably, the native of an area – and this is in no way meant to be condescending – tends to reject his local vegetation and long for someone else's, which to him is more desirable. This is basic human nature, Muslim as well as Christian; conversely the outsider finds the local vegetation of a place he visits very exciting. The European visiting desert areas of intense heat and drought is intrigued by the bizarre formations of cactus and succulent plants growing there, though the local no doubt finds them hostile. This very bizarreness is an expression of the way in which the plant adapts to its location, and the hostility of its form – its spikes and spines – was developed to deter predators. So, whether liked or not, cacti and succulents are the indigenous plants, though when growing naturally they do not compose themselves into the handsome arrangements which twentieth-century gardeners can achieve.

In conjunction with modern buildings in an arid landscape and with suitable accompanying rock groupings, these plants are admirably suited for inclusion in a garden setting. Care, however, has to be exercised as to where they are used, for the spines of many are quite lethal, and could be a danger to children playing nearby. For the same reason, however, cacti can be used as a deterrent, in public planting for instance; hedges of prickly pear are used to enclose livestock in various parts of the world, although this particular plant can become invasive.

SUBSEQUENT MAINTENANCE

We have tried to show in this section that it is possible to combine a traditional form with modern requirements, but it is impossible to give detailed steps for the establishment of a particular garden as the area is so vast and conditions so different. However, enough information has been presented to make the new garden builder aware of both the precedents and the problems, and enough to show the folly of trying to create a Western garden pattern in an environment that is hostile to such a form, especially an environment evolved out of another philosophy and way of life. Each landscape hosts its own garden vernacular, as it has produced its architecture and life-style for those who live there – they are as much a part of the landscape as the plants which grow upon it.

No garden is static; it needs maintenance and care. Those gardens which are at one with their landscape, that is, use local materials hard or soft, will mature along natural lines and will need less attention. Those which incorporate alien characteristics will need more detailed looking after. While there is an increasing awareness of horticultural techniques in the Middle East, there is no tradition of gardening as such. Local labour can be trained to carry out day-to-day functions, but without the knowledge of specialist plant materials and the broader concepts of water conservation, wind-break planting and plant preservation the best-planned scheme is doomed to failure. It is necessary therefore for the owner, if he has had his garden designed, to understand the designer's concept and, if no maintenance contractor has been retained, to direct the day-to-day maintenance of the garden himself, so that it ultimately becomes his own particular form of earthly paradise.

CHRONOLOGY

Garden names and/or their locations are given in italics.

DATE	PERSIA	SPAIN	INDIA	OTHER REGIONS
591–628	Reign of Sassanian monarch Khusraw II *Imarat-i Khusraw at Qasr-i Shirin*			
632				Death of the Prophet Muhammad at Medina (Arabia)
636–642	Muslim conquest			
640–642				Muslim conquest of Egypt
661–750	Umayyad khalifate			Umayyad khalifate (based at Damascus, Syria)
711		Muslim invasion		Muslim rule in North Africa
732				Fall of Avignon and Poitiers marks limit of Muslim advance in Europe
750–1258	Abbasid khalifate			Abbasid khalifate (based at Baghdad, Iraq)
756–1031		Umayyad period		
785–987		*Great Mosque, Cordoba (Patio de los Naranjos)*		
800–909				Aghlabid period (Tunisia and eastern Algeria)
827				Aghlabid conquest of Sicily
836–892				Samarra (Iraq) becomes Abbasid capital *Jawsaq al-Khaqani, Samarra*
849–859				*Bulkawara Palace, Samarra*
909–1171				Fatimid period (North Africa and, from 969, Egypt)
932–1062	Buyid period (capital: Shiraz)			
935–68				Ikshidid period (Egypt) *Garden of Kafur, nr Fustat*
936		*Madinat al-Zahra, nr Cordoba, founded*		
1030–1081		*Aljaferia, Zaragoza*		

DATE	PERSIA	SPAIN	INDIA	OTHER REGIONS
1038–1194	Saljuq period *Bagh-i Bakr, Bagh-i Falasan and Bagh-i Karan, Isfahan*			
1056–1147				Almoravid period (North Africa)
1086–1147		Almoravid period		
1130–1269		Almohad period		Almohad period (North Africa)
1171–1250				Ayyubid period (Egypt)
1196–1549				Marinid period (Morocco)
1206			Sultanate established in Delhi	
1238–1492		Nasrid period in Granada		
1250–1517				Mamluk period (Egypt)
1256–1353	Mongol period			
1294–1304	Reign of Mahmud Ghazan Khan *Gardens at Ujan and Sham, nr Tabriz*			
c. 1300–1924				Ottoman empire (Turkey)
1319		*Generalife, Granada*		
1310–59				*Chellah, Rabat, Morocco*
1350–55				*Bou Inaniye Medersa, Fez, Morocco*
1354–91		Reign of Muhammad V in Granada *Alhambra (Courts of Myrtles and Lions), Granada*		
1364		*Alcazar, Seville (rebuilt)*		
1370–1506	Timurid period			
1396	*Bagh-i Dilgusha and Bagh-i Shimal, Samarkand*			
1398			Timur's invasion	
1404	*Gul Bagh, Samarkand*			
1405	Death of Timur			
1425	*Gazur Gah (shrine), Herat*			
1437	*Shrine of Nimatullah, Mahan, begun*			
1453				Ottomans take Constantinople

DATE	PERSIA	SPAIN	INDIA	OTHER REGIONS
1483		Casa de las Duenas, Seville		
1501–1732	Safavid period			
1504	Babur takes Kabul *Bagh-i Vafa, Kabul*			
1517–1805				Ottoman period (Egypt and much of North Africa)
1526–1858			Mughal period	
1526			Ram Bagh, Agra	
1543				*Takiyya of Sultan Sulayman II, Cairo, Egypt*
1556			Death of Humayun	
1556–1605			Reign of Akbar *Nasim Bagh, Kashmir (after 1597)*	
1565–72			*Tomb of Humayun, Delhi*	
1571–80			*Fathpur Sikri*	
c.1570			*Jahangiri Mahal, Agra*	
1586			Mughal conquest of Kashmir	
1587–1629	Reign of Shah Abbas I *Shrine of Nimatullah, Mahan, enlarged*			
1590	*Bagh-i Fin, Kashan*			
1597			*Hari Parbat, Kashmir*	
1598	Isfahan becomes Safavid capital			
1598–1612	*Ali Qapu, Isfahan (renovated)*			
1604–13			*Tomb of Akbar, Sikandra*	
1605–27			Reign of Jahangir *Achabal, Kashmir*	
1609–12				*Ahmediye Mosque (Blue Mosque), Constantinople*
1609			*Verinag, Kashmir*	
1612–38	*Masjid-i Shah Mosque, Isfahan*			
1619			*Shalamar Bagh, Kashmir*	
1622–8			*Tomb of Itimad al-Daulah, Agra*	
1625			*Nishat Bagh, Kashmir*	

DATE	PERSIA	SPAIN	INDIA	OTHER REGIONS
1628–58			Reign of Shah Jahan *Peri Mahal, Kashmir* *Red Fort, Agra*	
1632			*Chasma Shahi,* *Kashmir*	
1635				*Revan Kiosk, Topkapi,* *Constantinople*
1632–54			*Taj Mahal, Agra*	
1638–48			*Red Fort, Delhi*	
1643			*Shalamar Bagh,* *Lahore*	
1646–54			*Moti Masjid, Red Fort,* *Agra*	
1647	*Chehel Sutun, Isfahan* (*completed*)			
1658–1707			Reign of Aurangzeb	
1662			*Pearl Mosque, Delhi*	
1670	*Hasht Behist, Isfahan*			
1706–14	*Madrasa Madar-i* *Shah, Isfahan*			
1736–47	Reign of Nadir Shah			
1750				*Takiyya of Sultan* *Mahmud II, Cairo*
1750–79	Reign of Karim Khan Zand *Bagh-i Dilgusha, Haft* *Tan and Chehil Tan in* *Shiraz* (*the new capital*)			
1779–1924	Qajar period			
1785 and 19th century	*Shah Gul, Tabriz*			
c.1789	*Bagh-i Takht, Shiraz*			
1799–1834	Reign of Fath Ali Shah *Bagh-i Fin renovated*			
1805–1953				Muhammad Ali period (Egypt)
1806	*Gulistan Palace,* *Tehran*			
1810	*Negaristan Palace,* *Tehran*			
1824	*Bagh-i Eram, Shiraz*			
1840s	*Shrine of Nimatullah,* *nr Mahan, added to*			
1870s	*Naranjistan, Shiraz*			
Last half of 19th century	*Farman Farma, nr* *Mahan*			

SELECT BIBLIOGRAPHY

GENERAL

Islam and Islamic Architecture
Nadar Ardalan and Laleh Bakhtiar, *The Sense of Unity,* University of Chicago
    Press 1975
Alfred Guillaume, *Islam,* Pelican 1975
John D. Hoag, *Western Islamic Architecture,* Studio Vista 1968
The Koran, translated by N. J. Dawood, Penguin Classics 1966
Reuben Levy, *The Social Structure of Islam,* Cambridge University Press 1962
George Michell (ed.), *Architecture of the Islamic World,* Thames and Hudson 1978

Histories of Islamic Gardens
Jonas Lehrman, *Earthly Paradise: Garden and Courtyard in Islam,* University of
    California Press 1980
Elizabeth B. MacDougall and Richard Ettinghausen (eds.), *The Islamic Garden,*
    Dumbarton Oaks (Harvard University Press) 1976
Elizabeth B. Moynihan, *Paradise as a Garden in Persia and Mughal India,* George
    Braziller 1979

PERSIA

General
Warwick Ball and Antony Hutt, *Persian Landscape,* Scorpion 1978
Alessandro Bausani, *The Persians,* Elek Books 1975
Anthony Smith, *Blind White Fish of Persia,* Unwin 1966
Donald N. Wilber, *Contemporary Iran,* Thames and Hudson 1963

History
Wilfrid Blunt and Wim Swaan, *Isfahan: Pearl of Persia,* Elek Books 1966
Richard N. Frye, *The Heritage of Persia,* Mentor 1963
Antony Hutt and Len Harrow, *Iran I,* Scorpion 1977
Antony Hutt and Len Harrow, *Iran II,* Scorpion 1978
Sylvia Matheson, *Persia, An Archaeological Guide,* Faber and Faber 1972
Arthur Upham Pope, *Persian Architecture,* Oxford University Press 1969
Roger Stevens, *Land of the Great Sophy,* Methuen 1971

Gardens
William L. Hanaway, *Paradise on Earth: The Terrestrial Garden in Persian Litera-
    ture,* Dumbarton Oaks 1976
Ralph Pinder-Wilson, 'The Persian Garden: *Bagh* and *Chahar Bagh*', a paper
    delivered to Dumbarton Oaks 1976
Donald N. Wilber, *Persian Gardens and Garden Pavilions,* Charles E. Tuttle 1962

SPAIN

James Dickie, 'The Hispano-Arab Garden', in the *Bulletin of the School of Oriental and African Studies* Vol. 31 (1968)
James Dickie, 'The Islamic Garden in Spain', in *The Islamic Garden,* edited by Elizabeth MacDougall and Richard Ettinghausen, Dumbarton Oaks 1976
Oleg Grabar, *The Alhambra,* Allen Lane 1978
Jardines de España, Casa Valdes, Aguilar 1973
Francisco Prieto-Moreno, *Los Jardines de Granada,* Editorial Cigueña 1952
Desmond Stewart, *The Alhambra: A History of Islamic Spain,* Newsweek 1974
C. M. Villiers-Stuart, *Spanish Gardens,* Batsford 1936

INDIA

Percy Brown, *Indian Architecture: Islamic Period,* Taraporevala 1964
Sylvia Crowe, Sheila Haywood and Susan Jellicoe, *The Gardens of Mughul India,* Thames and Hudson 1972
Bamber Gascoigne, *The Great Moghuls,* Jonathan Cape 1973
Susan Jellicoe, 'The Development of the Mughul Garden', a paper delivered to Dumbarton Oaks 1976
C. M. Villiers-Stuart, *Gardens of the Great Mughals,* A. & C. Black 1913

NORTH AFRICA

Antony Hutt, *North Africa,* Scorpion 1977

TURKEY

Godfrey Goodwin, *Ottoman Turkey,* Scorpion 1977

ARABIA

R. and M. Adams and A. and A. Willens, *Dry Lands: Man and Plants,* Architectural Press 1978
Timothy Cochrane and Jane Brown (eds.), *Landscape Design for the Middle East,* RIBA Publications 1977
Kathleen Kelly and R. T. Schnadelbach, *Landscaping the Saudi Arabian Desert,* Delancey Press 1976

INDEX

Page numbers in *italic* refer to illustrations and plans

237

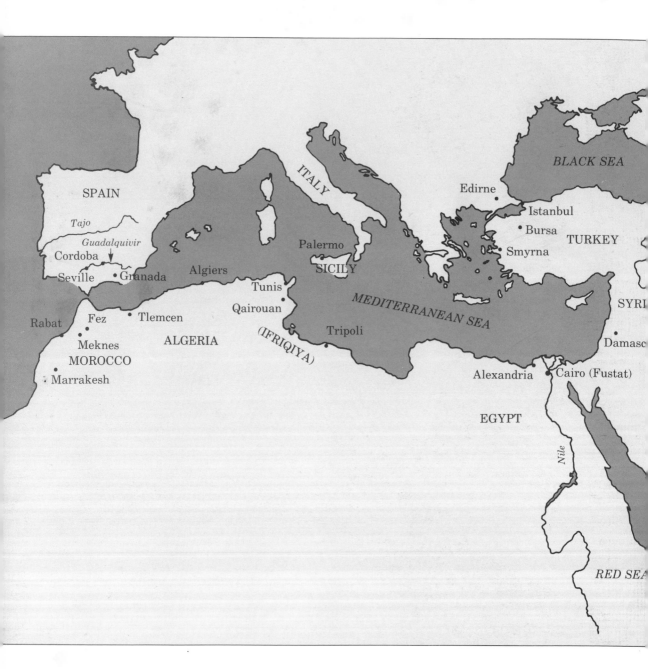

THE ISLAMIC WORLD AND GARDEN LOCATIONS
(*former names are given in brackets*).